CLASSIC DESSERTS

Eagle® Brand Sweetened Condensed Milk

PUBLICATIONS INTERNATIONAL, LTD.

CONTENTS

© 1986 Borden, Inc.

Eagle® is a registered trademark of
Borden, Inc.

Recipe Development:
   Borden Kitchens
   Annie Watts Cloncs, Director
   Charlene Sneed, Senior Home Economist

Photography Coordination:
Mallard Marketing Associates, Inc.

Library of Congress Catalog Card
Number: 86-60771

ISBN: 0-88176-865-0

Pictured on the front cover: *New York Style
Cheesecake* (page 24).

Pictured on back cover, counterclockwise
from top: *Creamy Lemon Meringue Pie*
(page 6), *Layered Mint Chocolate Candy*
(page 83), *Fruit Bon Bons* (page 81),
Scotchy Pecan Critters (page 80), *Mini
Fruitcake Morsels* (page 47), *Peanut
Blossoms* (page 38) and *Triple Layer
Cookie Bars* (page 43).

Printed and bound in Tiskarna Slovenija,
Yugoslavia
10   9   8   7   6   5   4   3   2   1

CLASSIC DESSERTS...
TODAY'S EASY WAY

For nearly 130 years, Eagle® Brand Sweetened Condensed Milk has been a trusted product with American consumers. Developed by Gail Borden in 1856 to provide wholesome milk which could be stored unrefrigerated, sweetened condensed milk was originally used as an all-purpose milk—infant formula, coffee sweetener and creamer, and for all types of cooking. Today, Eagle Brand's all natural precooked blend of whole milk and pure cane sugar provides the convenient, high quality base for hundreds of delicious desserts. In fact, it's been called "magic"...a can of Eagle® Brand Sweetened Condensed Milk plus a few select ingredients and the results are, well, like magic! Rich chocolate candies, moist cookie bars, picture-perfect pies, luscious cheesecakes, fudgy frostings, caramel flans and creamy smooth ice creams...just a few of the classic desserts from Eagle Brand. These recipes were developed by the home economists of the Borden Kitchens to assure you the easy preparation, good taste and high quality that American cooks have come to expect from Eagle Brand— today's easy way to homemade desserts!

PIES

With the "magic" of Eagle Brand, create family-favorite and party-perfect pies with little or no cooking! Choose from ever-popular Cherry Cheese, easy Creamy Lemon Meringue, rich Fudgy Pecan or Traditional Pumpkin, all made in minutes, easily with Eagle Brand.

CHERRY CHEESE PIE

Makes one 9-inch pie

1 (9-inch) baked pastry shell *or* graham cracker crumb crust
1 (8-ounce) package cream cheese, softened
1 (14-ounce) can Eagle® Brand Sweetened Condensed Milk (NOT evaporated milk)
⅓ cup ReaLemon® Lemon Juice from Concentrate
1 teaspoon vanilla extract
1 (21-ounce) can cherry pie filling, chilled

In large mixer bowl, beat cheese until fluffy. Gradually beat in sweetened condensed milk until smooth. Stir in ReaLemon and vanilla. Pour into prepared pastry shell. Chill 3 hours or until set. Top with desired amount of pie filling before serving. Refrigerate leftovers.

Topping Variations:

Ambrosia: Omit cherry pie filling. In small saucepan, combine ½ cup peach *or* apricot preserves, ¼ cup flaked coconut, 2 tablespoons orange juice *or* orange-flavored liqueur and 2 teaspoons cornstarch; cook and stir until thickened. Remove from heat. Arrange fresh orange sections over top of pie; top with coconut mixture. Chill thoroughly.

Fresh Fruit: Omit cherry pie filling. Just before serving, arrange well drained fresh strawberries, banana slices (dipped in ReaLemon and well drained) and blueberries on top of chilled pie. Just before serving, brush fruit with light corn syrup if desired.

Cranberry: Omit cherry pie filling. In medium saucepan, combine ⅓ cup sugar and 1 tablespoon cornstarch. Add ½ cup plus 2 tablespoons cold water and 2 cups fresh or dry-pack frozen cranberries; mix well. Bring to a boil; reduce heat and simmer 10 minutes, stirring constantly. Cool 15 minutes. Spread over pie. Chill thoroughly.

MILLION DOLLAR PIES

Makes two 8-inch pies

2 (8-inch) prepared graham cracker crumb crusts
1 (3½-ounce) can flaked coconut (1⅓ cups)
1 (14-ounce) can Eagle® Brand Sweetened Condensed Milk (NOT evaporated milk)
1 (20-ounce) can juice-pack crushed pineapple *or* 1 (29-ounce) can fruit cocktail, *well drained*
1 cup coarsely chopped pecans
¼ cup ReaLemon® Lemon Juice from Concentrate
1 (8-ounce) container frozen non-dairy whipped topping, thawed

Toast ⅓ *cup* coconut; set aside. In large mixing bowl, combine sweetened condensed milk, pineapple, remaining *1 cup* coconut, pecans and ReaLemon; mix well. Fold in whipped topping. Pour into prepared crusts. Garnish with toasted coconut. Chill 3 hours or until set. Refrigerate leftovers.

Cherry Cheese Pie (top), Ambrosia Cheese Pie (bottom)

CREAMY LEMON MERINGUE PIE

Makes one 8- or 9-inch pie

1 (8- or 9-inch) baked pastry shell *or* graham cracker crumb crust
3 eggs,* separated
1 (14-ounce) can Eagle® Brand Sweetened Condensed Milk (NOT evaporated milk)
½ cup ReaLemon® Lemon Juice from Concentrate
Few drops yellow food coloring, optional
¼ teaspoon cream of tartar
⅓ cup sugar

Preheat oven to 350°. In medium mixing bowl, beat egg yolks; stir in sweetened condensed milk, ReaLemon and food coloring if desired. Pour into prepared pastry shell. In small mixer bowl, beat egg whites with cream of tartar until soft peaks form; gradually add sugar, beating until stiff but not dry. Spread meringue on top of pie, sealing carefully to edge of shell. Bake 12 to 15 minutes or until golden brown. Cool. Chill thoroughly. Refrigerate leftovers.

*Use only Grade A clean, uncracked eggs.

IMPOSSIBLE PIE

Makes one 10-inch pie

1 (14-ounce) can Eagle® Brand Sweetened Condensed Milk (NOT evaporated milk)
1½ cups water
½ cup biscuit baking mix
3 eggs
¼ cup margarine or butter, softened
1½ teaspoons vanilla extract
1 cup flaked coconut

Preheat oven to 350°. In blender container, combine all ingredients except coconut. Blend on low speed 3 minutes. Pour mixture into buttered 10-inch pie plate; let stand 5 minutes. Sprinkle coconut over top. Carefully place in oven; bake 35 to 40 minutes or until knife inserted near edge comes out clean. Cool slightly; serve warm or cool. Refrigerate leftovers.

Tip: Pie can be baked in buttered 9-inch pie plate but it will be extremely full.

Creamy Lemon Meringue Pie

FUDGY PECAN PIE ▲

Makes one 9-inch pie

1 (9-inch) unbaked pastry shell
1 (4-ounce) package sweet cooking
   chocolate *or* 2 (1-ounce) squares
   unsweetened chocolate
¼ cup margarine or butter
1 (14-ounce) can Eagle® Brand
   Sweetened Condensed Milk
   (NOT evaporated milk)
½ cup hot water
2 eggs, well beaten
1 teaspoon vanilla extract
⅛ teaspoon salt
1¼ cups pecan halves or pieces

Preheat oven to 350°. In medium saucepan,
over low heat, melt chocolate with margarine.
Stir in sweetened condensed milk, hot water
and eggs; *mix well*. Remove from heat; stir in
remaining ingredients. Pour into prepared
pastry shell. Bake 40 to 45 minutes or until
center is set. Cool slightly. Serve warm or
chilled. Garnish as desired. Refrigerate
leftovers.

FUDGE DELUXE PIE

Makes one 9-inch pie

1 (9-inch) baked pastry shell
3 (1-ounce) squares semi-sweet *or*
   unsweetened chocolate
1 (14-ounce) can Eagle® Brand
   Sweetened Condensed Milk
   (NOT evaporated milk)
¼ teaspoon salt
¼ cup hot water
1 teaspoon vanilla extract
1 cup (½ pint) whipping cream

In heavy saucepan, over medium heat, melt
chocolate with sweetened condensed milk and
salt. Cook and stir until very thick and fudgy, 5
to 8 minutes. Add water; cook and stir until
mixture thickens and boils. Remove from heat;
stir in vanilla. Cool 15 minutes. Chill
thoroughly, 20 to 30 minutes; stir. In large
mixer bowl, beat whipping cream until stiff;
fold in cooled chocolate mixture. Pour into
prepared pastry shell. Chill 3 hours or until
set. Garnish as desired. Refrigerate leftovers.

TRADITIONAL PUMPKIN PIE ▶

Makes one 9-inch pie

1 (9-inch) unbaked pastry shell
1 (16-ounce) can pumpkin (about
    2 cups)
1 (14-ounce) can Eagle® Brand
    Sweetened Condensed Milk
    (NOT evaporated milk)
2 eggs
1 teaspoon ground cinnamon
½ teaspoon ground ginger
½ teaspoon ground nutmeg
½ teaspoon salt

Preheat oven to 425°. In large mixer bowl,
combine all ingredients except pastry shell;
mix well. Pour into prepared pastry shell.
Bake 15 minutes. Reduce oven temperature to
350°; continue baking 35 to 40 minutes or until
knife inserted 1 inch from edge comes out
clean. Cool. Garnish as desired. Refrigerate
leftovers.

Topping Variations:

Sour Cream Topping: In medium mixing
bowl, combine 1½ cups sour cream, 2
tablespoons sugar and 1 teaspoon vanilla
extract. After 30 minutes of baking, spread
evenly over top of pie; bake 10 minutes longer.
Garnish as desired.

Streusel Topping: In medium mixing bowl,
combine ½ cup firmly packed light brown
sugar and ½ cup unsifted flour; cut in ¼ cup
cold margarine or butter until crumbly. Stir in
¼ cup chopped nuts. After 30 minutes of
baking, sprinkle on top of pie; bake 10 minutes
longer.

LEMON CHIFFON PIE

Makes one 8- or 9-inch pie

1 (8- or 9-inch) graham cracker crumb
    crust
1 (14-ounce) can Eagle® Brand
    Sweetened Condensed Milk
    (NOT evaporated milk)
⅓ cup ReaLemon® Lemon Juice from
    Concentrate
    Few drops yellow food coloring,
    optional
3 egg whites*
¼ teaspoon cream of tartar

In medium mixing bowl, combine sweetened
condensed milk, ReaLemon and food coloring if
desired; mix well. In small mixer bowl, beat
egg whites with cream of tartar until stiff but
not dry; gently fold into sweetened condensed
milk mixture. Pour into prepared crust. Chill 3
hours or until set. Refrigerate leftovers.

*Use only Grade A clean, uncracked eggs.

LEMON ICEBOX PIE

Makes one 9-inch pie

1½ cups vanilla wafer crumbs (about
    40 wafers)
¼ cup margarine or butter, melted
1 envelope unflavored gelatine
1¾ cups water
1 (14-ounce) can Eagle® Brand
    Sweetened Condensed Milk
    (NOT evaporated milk)
1 (3-ounce) package *or* 6 tablespoons
    Wyler's® Presweetened Lemonade
    Flavor Drink Crystals

Combine crumbs and margarine; press firmly
on bottom and up side of 9-inch pie plate. Chill.
Meanwhile, in small saucepan, sprinkle
gelatine over *¼ cup* water; let stand 1 minute.
Over low heat, stir until gelatine dissolves; set
aside. In medium mixing bowl, combine
sweetened condensed milk, remaining *1½ cups*
water and lemonade crystals; mix well. Stir in
gelatine mixture. Pour into prepared crust.
Chill at least 3 hours or until set. Garnish as
desired. Refrigerate leftovers.

PINK LEMONADE PIE

Makes one 8- or 9-inch pie

1 (8- or 9-inch) baked pastry shell
1 (6-ounce) can frozen pink lemonade
    concentrate, thawed
1 (8-ounce) package cream cheese,
    softened
1 (14-ounce) can Eagle® Brand
    Sweetened Condensed Milk
    (NOT evaporated milk)
   Few drops red food coloring, optional
1 (4-ounce) container frozen non-dairy
    whipped topping, thawed
½ cup pink tinted coconut*

In large mixer bowl, beat cheese until fluffy;
gradually beat in sweetened condensed milk
then lemonade concentrate and food coloring if
desired. Fold in whipped topping. Pour into
prepared pastry shell. Chill 4 hours or until
set. Garnish with coconut. Refrigerate
leftovers.

*See page 91.

TROPICAL LIME PIE ▲

Makes one 9-inch pie

2½ cups flaked coconut, toasted
⅓ cup margarine or butter, melted
1 (8-ounce) package cream cheese, softened
1 (14-ounce) can Eagle® Brand Sweetened Condensed Milk (NOT evaporated milk)
⅓ cup ReaLime® Lime Juice from Concentrate
   Few drops green food coloring, optional
1 (4-ounce) container frozen non-dairy whipped topping, thawed

Combine coconut and margarine; press firmly on bottom and up side to rim of 9-inch pie plate. Chill. Meanwhile, in large mixer bowl, beat cheese until fluffy. Gradually beat in sweetened condensed milk then ReaLime and food coloring if desired until smooth. Fold in whipped topping. Pour into prepared crust. Chill 3 hours or until set. Garnish as desired. Refrigerate leftovers.

CREAMY MOCK CHEESE PIE

Makes one 8- or 9-inch pie

1 (8- or 9-inch) graham cracker crumb crust
1 (16-ounce) container sour cream
1 (14-ounce) can Eagle® Brand Sweetened Condensed Milk (NOT evaporated milk)
3 tablespoons (1 scoop) Wyler's® Presweetened Lemonade Flavor Drink Crystals
   Peach preserves, optional

Preheat oven to 350°. In medium mixing bowl, combine sour cream, sweetened condensed milk and lemonade crystals; mix well. Pour into prepared crust. Bake 25 to 30 minutes. Cool thoroughly. Chill at least 2 hours. Garnish with preserves if desired. Refrigerate leftovers.

Tip: Other fruit preserves can be substituted for peach preserves.

FLUFFY ORANGE PIE

Makes one 9-inch pie

- 2 cups vanilla wafer crumbs (about 50 wafers)
- ⅓ cup margarine or butter, melted
- 1 (8-ounce) package cream cheese, softened
- 1 (14-ounce) can Eagle® Brand Sweetened Condensed Milk (NOT evaporated milk)
- 1 (6-ounce) can frozen orange juice concentrate, thawed
- 1 cup (½ pint) whipping cream, whipped

Combine crumbs and margarine; press firmly on bottom and up side of 9-inch pie plate. Chill. Meanwhile, in large mixer bowl, beat cheese until fluffy; gradually beat in sweetened condensed milk then juice concentrate until smooth. Fold in whipped cream. Pile into crust. Chill 2 hours or until set. Garnish as desired. Refrigerate leftovers.

AVOCADO CHEESE PIE

Makes one 9-inch pie

- 1 (9-inch) graham cracker crumb crust
- 1 (8-ounce) package cream cheese, softened
- 1 (14-ounce) can Eagle® Brand Sweetened Condensed Milk (NOT evaporated milk)
- 1 ripe medium avocado, mashed or pureed (about ½ cup)
- ½ cup ReaLime® Lime Juice from Concentrate
- ¼ teaspoon salt
  Few drops green food coloring, optional
  Whipped cream, optional

In large mixer bowl, beat cheese until fluffy. Gradually beat in sweetened condensed milk then avocado, ReaLime, salt and food coloring if desired until smooth. Pour into prepared crust. Chill 4 hours or until set. Garnish with whipped cream if desired. Refrigerate leftovers.

Fluffy Orange Pie

◀ MINI FRUIT CHEESE TARTS

Makes 24 tarts

24 (2- or 3-inch) prepared tart-size crusts
1 (8-ounce) package cream cheese, softened
1 (14-ounce) can Eagle® Brand Sweetened Condensed Milk (NOT evaporated milk)
⅓ cup ReaLemon® Lemon Juice from Concentrate
1 teaspoon vanilla extract
   Assorted fruit (strawberries, blueberries, bananas, raspberries, orange segments, cherries, kiwifruit, grapes, pineapple, etc.)
¼ cup apple jelly, melted

In large mixer bowl, beat cheese until fluffy. Gradually beat in sweetened condensed milk until smooth. Stir in ReaLemon and vanilla. Spoon equal portions into crusts. Top with fruit; brush with jelly. Chill thoroughly. Refrigerate leftovers.

SPIRITED EGG NOG CUSTARD PIE

Makes one 9-inch pie

1 (9-inch) unbaked pastry shell
1 (14-ounce) can Eagle® Brand Sweetened Condensed Milk (NOT evaporated milk)
1⅓ cups warm water
2 tablespoons light rum
1 tablespoon brandy
1 teaspoon vanilla extract
½ teaspoon ground nutmeg
3 eggs, well beaten

Preheat oven to 425°. Bake pastry shell 8 minutes; remove from oven. In large mixing bowl, combine all ingredients except eggs; mix well. Stir in eggs. Pour into prepared pastry shell. Bake 10 minutes. Reduce oven temperature to 325°; continue baking 25 to 30 minutes or until knife inserted near center comes out clean. Cool. Chill if desired. Refrigerate leftovers.

COCONUT CUSTARD PIE ▲

Makes one 9-inch pie

1 (9-inch) unbaked pastry shell
1 cup flaked coconut
3 eggs
1 (14-ounce) can Eagle® Brand
    Sweetened Condensed Milk
    (NOT evaporated milk)
1¼ cups hot water
1 teaspoon vanilla extract
¼ teaspoon salt
⅛ teaspoon ground nutmeg

Preheat oven to 425°. Toast ½ cup coconut; set aside. Bake pastry shell 8 minutes; cool slightly. Meanwhile, in medium mixing bowl, beat eggs. Add sweetened condensed milk, water, vanilla, salt and nutmeg; mix well. Stir in remaining ½ cup coconut. Pour into prepared pastry shell. Sprinkle with toasted coconut. Bake 10 minutes. Reduce oven temperature to 350°; continue baking 25 to 30 minutes or until knife inserted near center comes out clean. Cool. Chill if desired. Refrigerate leftovers.

Custard Pie: Omit coconut. Proceed as above.

CHOCOLATE CUSTARD PIE

Makes one 9-inch pie

1 (9-inch) unbaked pastry shell
2 (1-ounce) squares semi-sweet
    chocolate
1 (14-ounce) can Eagle® Brand
    Sweetened Condensed Milk
    (NOT evaporated milk)
3 eggs, well beaten
1½ cups *hot* water
2 teaspoons vanilla extract
1 (4-ounce) container frozen non-dairy
    whipped topping, thawed

Preheat oven to 425°. In heavy saucepan, over low heat, melt chocolate with sweetened condensed milk. Stir in eggs; mix well. Add hot water and vanilla; mix well. Pour into prepared pastry shell. Bake 10 minutes. Reduce oven temperature to 300°; continue baking 25 to 30 minutes or until knife inserted near center comes out clean. Cool. Chill thoroughly. Spread top with whipped topping. Refrigerate leftovers.

Streusel-Topped Apple Custard Pie (top), Candy Apple Cheese Pie (bottom)

STREUSEL-TOPPED APPLE CUSTARD PIE

Makes one 9-inch pie

1 (9-inch) unbaked pastry shell
4 large all-purpose apples, pared and
    sliced (about 4 cups)
2 eggs
1 (14-ounce) can Eagle® Brand
    Sweetened Condensed Milk
    (NOT evaporated milk)
¼ cup margarine or butter, melted
½ teaspoon ground cinnamon
    Dash ground nutmeg
½ cup firmly packed light brown sugar
½ cup unsifted flour
¼ cup cold margarine or butter
¼ cup chopped nuts

Preheat oven to 425°. Arrange apples in prepared pastry shell. In medium mixing bowl, beat eggs. Add sweetened condensed milk, margarine, cinnamon and nutmeg; mix well. Pour over apples. In medium mixing bowl, combine sugar and flour; cut in margarine until crumbly. Stir in nuts. Sprinkle over pie. Place in bottom third of oven; bake 10 minutes. Reduce oven temperature to 375°; continue baking 35 to 40 minutes or until golden brown. Cool. Refrigerate leftovers.

Peach Variation: Omit apples. Substitute 1 (29-ounce) can sliced peaches, well drained, for apples. Proceed as above.

CANDY APPLE CHEESE PIE

Makes one 9-inch pie

1 (9-inch) baked pastry shell
1 (8-ounce) package cream cheese, softened
1 (14-ounce) can Eagle® Brand Sweetened Condensed Milk (NOT evaporated milk)
⅓ cup ReaLemon® Lemon Juice from Concentrate
1 teaspoon vanilla extract
1 (20-ounce) can pie sliced apples, *well drained* on paper towels
¼ cup red cinnamon candies
6 tablespoons water
2 teaspoons cornstarch

In large mixer bowl, beat cheese until fluffy. Gradually beat in sweetened condensed milk until smooth. Stir in ReaLemon and vanilla. Pour into prepared pastry shell. Arrange apple slices on top; set aside. In small saucepan, over *low* heat, dissolve cinnamon candies in *¼ cup* water. Stir together remaining *2 tablespoons* water and cornstarch; add to cinnamon mixture. Cook and stir until mixture thickens and boils. Remove from heat; cool slightly. Drizzle over apples. Chill 3 hours or until set. Refrigerate leftovers.

SPIRITED ALOHA CREAM PIE

Makes one 9-inch pie

2½ cups flaked coconut, toasted
⅓ cup margarine or butter, melted
1 (8-ounce) package cream cheese, softened
1 (14-ounce) can Eagle® Brand Sweetened Condensed Milk (NOT evaporated milk)
1 (6-ounce) can frozen pineapple-orange juice concentrate, thawed
1 (8-ounce) can crushed pineapple, well drained
3 tablespoons light rum
1 tablespoon orange-flavored liqueur
1 cup (½ pint) whipping cream, whipped

Combine coconut and margarine; press firmly on bottom and up side to rim of 9-inch pie plate. Chill. Meanwhile, in large mixer bowl, beat cheese until fluffy. Gradually beat in sweetened condensed milk then juice concentrate until smooth. Stir in pineapple, rum and liqueur. Fold in whipped cream. Pour into prepared crust. Chill 6 hours or until set. Garnish as desired. Refrigerate leftovers.

KEY LIME PIE

Makes one 8- or 9-inch pie

1 (8- or 9-inch) baked pastry shell
3 eggs,* separated
1 (14-ounce) can Eagle® Brand Sweetened Condensed Milk (NOT evaporated milk)
½ cup ReaLime® Lime Juice from Concentrate
Few drops green food coloring, optional
½ teaspoon cream of tartar
⅓ cup sugar

Preheat oven to 350°. In medium mixing bowl, beat egg yolks; stir in sweetened condensed milk, ReaLime and food coloring if desired. Pour into prepared pastry shell. In small mixer bowl, beat egg whites with cream of tartar until soft peaks form; gradually add sugar, beating until stiff but not dry. Spread on top of pie, sealing carefully to edge of shell. Bake 12 to 15 minutes or until golden brown. Cool. Chill thoroughly. Refrigerate leftovers.

Tip: For a lighter filling, fold 1 stiffly beaten egg white into filling mixture; proceed as above.

*Use only Grade A clean, uncracked eggs.

BANANA SPLIT DESSERT PIZZA

Makes one 12-inch pie

1 (14-ounce) can Eagle® Brand
    Sweetened Condensed Milk
    (NOT evaporated milk)
½ cup sour cream
6 tablespoons ReaLemon® Lemon Juice
    from Concentrate
1 teaspoon vanilla extract
½ cup margarine or butter, softened
¼ cup firmly packed brown sugar
1 cup unsifted flour
¾ cup chopped nuts
3 medium bananas, sliced
1 (8-ounce) can sliced pineapple,
    drained and cut in half
    Maraschino cherries and nuts
1 (1-ounce) square semi-sweet
    chocolate
1 tablespoon margarine or butter

Preheat oven to 375°. In medium mixing bowl, combine sweetened condensed milk, sour cream, ¼ cup ReaLemon and vanilla; mix well. Chill. In large mixer bowl, beat margarine and sugar until fluffy; add flour and ¾ cup nuts. Mix well. On lightly greased pizza pan or baking sheet, press dough into 12-inch circle forming rim around edge. Prick with fork. Bake 10 to 12 minutes or until golden brown. Cool. Arrange 2 bananas on cooled crust. Spoon filling evenly over bananas. Dip remaining banana slices in remaining 2 *tablespoons* ReaLemon; arrange on top along with pineapple, cherries and additional nuts. In small saucepan, over low heat, melt chocolate with margarine; drizzle over pie. Chill thoroughly. Refrigerate leftovers.

Tip: Crust and filling can be made in advance and held until ready to assemble. Cover crust and store at room temperature; store filling in refrigerator.

FLUFFY GRASSHOPPER PIE

Makes one 9-inch pie

- 2 cups finely crushed creme-filled chocolate sandwich cookies (about 20 cookies)
- ¼ cup margarine or butter, melted
- 1 (8-ounce) package cream cheese, softened
- 1 (14-ounce) can Eagle® Brand Sweetened Condensed Milk (NOT evaporated milk)
- 3 tablespoons ReaLemon® Lemon Juice from Concentrate
- ¼ cup green creme de menthe
- ¼ cup white creme de cacao
- 1 (4-ounce) container frozen non-dairy whipped topping, thawed *or* 1 cup (½ pint) whipping cream, stiffly whipped

Combine crumbs and margarine; press firmly on bottom and up side of buttered 9-inch pie plate. Chill. Meanwhile, in large mixer bowl, beat cheese until fluffy; gradually beat in sweetened condensed milk until smooth. Stir in ReaLemon and liqueurs. Fold in whipped topping. Chill 20 minutes; pile into crust. Chill or freeze 4 hours or until set. Garnish as desired. Refrigerate or freeze leftovers.

LUSCIOUS SWEET POTATO PIE

Makes one 9-inch pie

- 1 (9-inch) unbaked pastry shell
- 1 pound (2 medium) yams or sweet potatoes, cooked and peeled
- ½ cup margarine or butter, softened
- 1 (14-ounce) can Eagle® Brand Sweetened Condensed Milk (NOT evaporated milk)
- ¼ cup orange-flavored liqueur *or* 2 teaspoons grated orange rind
- 1 teaspoon ground cinnamon
- ½ teaspoon ground nutmeg
- ¼ teaspoon salt
- 2 eggs

Preheat oven to 350°. In large mixer bowl, mash yams with margarine; add remaining ingredients except pastry shell and eggs. Beat until mixture is smooth and well blended. Stir in eggs. Pour into prepared pastry shell. Bake 50 to 55 minutes or until knife inserted near center comes out clean. Cool. Refrigerate leftovers.

Tip: 1 (16- or 17-ounce) can sweet potatoes or yams can be substituted for fresh. Melt margarine. Proceed as above.

Fluffy Grasshopper Pie

GLAZED APPLE CREAM TART

Makes one 9-inch tart

½ cup plus 2 tablespoons margarine or butter, softened

¼ cup firmly packed light brown sugar

1 cup unsifted flour

¼ cup quick-cooking oats

¼ cup finely chopped walnuts

1 (14-ounce) can Eagle® Brand Sweetened Condensed Milk (NOT evaporated milk)

1 (16-ounce) container sour cream

½ cup frozen apple juice concentrate, thawed

2 eggs, beaten

1 teaspoon vanilla extract

2 medium all-purpose apples, pared and thinly sliced

½ cup apricot preserves

5 teaspoons water

1 teaspoon cornstarch

Preheat oven to 350°. In small mixer bowl, beat *½ cup* margarine and sugar until fluffy. Stir in flour, oats and nuts; press firmly on bottom and halfway up side of lightly greased 9-inch springform pan. Bake 15 to 20 minutes or until golden. Meanwhile, in medium mixing bowl, combine sweetened condensed milk and sour cream; add juice concentrate, eggs and vanilla. Mix well. Pour into prepared crust. Bake 30 to 35 minutes or until center is set. Cool. In medium saucepan, melt remaining *2 tablespoons* margarine. Add apples; cook and stir until tender. Arrange on top of tart. In small saucepan, combine preserves, water and cornstarch; cook and stir until preserves melt and mixture thickens slightly. Spoon over apples. Chill thoroughly. Refrigerate leftovers.

CRANBERRY CRUMB PIE ▲

Makes one 9-inch pie

1 (9-inch) unbaked pastry shell
1 (8-ounce) package cream cheese,
    softened
1 (14-ounce) can Eagle® Brand
    Sweetened Condensed Milk
    (NOT evaporated milk)
¼ cup ReaLemon® Lemon Juice from
    Concentrate
3 tablespoons light brown sugar
2 tablespoons cornstarch
1 (16-ounce) can whole berry cranberry
    sauce
¼ cup cold margarine or butter
⅓ cup unsifted flour
¾ cup chopped walnuts

Preheat oven to 425°. Bake pastry shell 8
minutes; remove from oven. Reduce oven
temperature to 375°. In large mixer bowl, beat
cheese until fluffy. Gradually beat in
sweetened condensed milk until smooth. Stir
in ReaLemon. Pour into prepared pastry shell.
In small bowl, combine *1 tablespoon* sugar and
cornstarch; mix well. Stir in cranberry sauce.
Spoon evenly over cheese mixture. In medium
mixing bowl, cut margarine into flour and
remaining *2 tablespoons* sugar until crumbly.
Stir in nuts. Sprinkle evenly over cranberry
mixture. Bake 45 to 50 minutes or until bubbly
and golden. Cool. Serve at room temperature or
chill thoroughly. Refrigerate leftovers.

FRESH FRUIT DESSERT PIZZA

Makes one 12-inch pie

1 (14-ounce) can Eagle® Brand
    Sweetened Condensed Milk
    (NOT evaporated milk)
½ cup sour cream
¼ cup ReaLemon® Lemon Juice from
    Concentrate
1 teaspoon vanilla extract
½ cup margarine or butter, softened
¼ cup firmly packed light brown sugar
1 cup unsifted flour
¼ cup quick-cooking oats
¼ cup finely chopped walnuts
    Assorted fresh or canned fruit
    (strawberries, grapes, kiwifruit,
    orange, pineapple, banana, etc.)

Preheat oven to 375°. In medium mixing bowl,
combine sweetened condensed milk, sour
cream, ReaLemon and vanilla; mix well. Chill.
In large mixer bowl, beat margarine and sugar
until fluffy; add flour, oats and walnuts. Mix
well. On lightly greased pizza pan or baking
sheet, press dough into 12-inch circle forming
rim around edge. Prick with fork. Bake 10 to 12
minutes or until golden brown. Cool. Spoon
filling evenly over crust. Arrange fruit on top.
Chill before serving. Refrigerate leftovers.

CAKES & CHEESECAKES

With Eagle Brand, you can easily create America's favorite restaurant dessert—cheesecake—at home. Choose from rich baked cheesecakes—New York Style, Chocolate Chip, even Butterscotch—or cool, creamy no-bake versions. Fresh fruit cakes, sheet cakes, ice cream cakes, step-by-step party cakes—all are featured here.

◄COOL AND MINTY PARTY CAKE

Makes one 9-inch cake

1 (14-ounce) can Eagle® Brand Sweetened Condensed Milk (NOT evaporated milk)
2 teaspoons peppermint extract
8 drops green food coloring
2 cups (1 pint) whipping cream, whipped *(do not use non-dairy whipped topping)*
1 (18¼- or 18½-ounce) package white cake mix
Green creme de menthe
1 (8-ounce) container frozen non-dairy whipped topping, thawed

In large mixing bowl, combine sweetened condensed milk, extract and food coloring. Fold in whipped cream. Pour into aluminum foil-lined 9-inch round layer cake pan; cover. Freeze at least 6 hours or overnight. Meanwhile, prepare and bake cake mix as package directs for two 9-inch round layers. Remove from pans; cool thoroughly. With table fork, poke holes in layers 1 inch apart halfway through each layer. Spoon small amounts of creme de menthe in holes. Place 1 cake layer on serving plate; top with ice cream layer then second cake layer. Trim ice cream layer to fit cake layers. Frost quickly with topping. Return to freezer until ready to serve. Garnish as desired.

Tip: Cake can be made 1 week ahead and stored in freezer.

NO-BAKE CHOCOLATE CHEESECAKE

Makes one 9-inch cheesecake

⅓ cup margarine or butter, melted
1¼ cups graham cracker crumbs
¼ cup sugar
1 envelope unflavored gelatine
⅔ cup water
2 (8-ounce) packages cream cheese, softened
4 (1-ounce) squares semi-sweet chocolate, melted
1 (14-ounce) can Eagle® Brand Sweetened Condensed Milk (NOT evaporated milk)
1 teaspoon vanilla extract
1 cup (½ pint) whipping cream, whipped

Combine margarine, crumbs and sugar; press firmly on bottom of 9-inch springform pan. In small saucepan, sprinkle gelatine over water; let stand 1 minute. Over low heat, stir until gelatine dissolves; set aside. In large mixer bowl, beat cheese and chocolate until fluffy. Gradually beat in sweetened condensed milk and vanilla until smooth. Stir in gelatine mixture. Fold in whipped cream. Pour into prepared pan. Chill 3 hours or until set. Garnish as desired. Refrigerate leftovers.

NEW YORK STYLE MARBLED CHEESECAKE

Makes one 9-inch cheesecake

⅓ cup margarine or butter, melted
1¼ cups graham cracker crumbs
¼ cup sugar
4 (8-ounce) packages cream cheese, softened
1 (14-ounce) can Eagle® Brand Sweetened Condensed Milk (NOT evaporated milk)
4 eggs
⅓ cup unsifted flour
1 tablespoon vanilla extract
2 to 4 (1-ounce) squares semi-sweet chocolate, melted

Preheat oven to 350°. Combine margarine, crumbs and sugar; press firmly on bottom of 9-inch springform pan. In large mixer bowl, beat cheese until fluffy. Gradually beat in sweetened condensed milk until smooth. Beat in eggs then flour and vanilla. Measure 1½ cups batter into medium mixing bowl. Add melted chocolate; mix well. Spoon half the yellow batter into prepared pan then half the chocolate batter. Repeat, ending with chocolate. With metal spatula, cut through batter to marble cake. Bake 1 hour or until lightly browned around edge. Cool to room temperature. Chill at least 6 hours. Garnish as desired. Refrigerate leftovers.

Tip: For best marbled effect, do not oversoften or overbeat cream cheese.

TEX-MEX SHEET CAKE ▶

Makes one 15×10-inch cake

1¼ cups margarine or butter
½ cup unsweetened cocoa
2 tablespoons instant coffee
1 cup water
2 cups unsifted flour
1½ cups firmly packed light brown sugar
1 teaspoon baking soda
1 teaspoon ground cinnamon
½ teaspoon salt
1 (14-ounce) can Eagle® Brand
    Sweetened Condensed Milk
    (NOT evaporated milk)
2 eggs
1 teaspoon vanilla extract
1 cup confectioners' sugar
1 cup toasted slivered almonds or
    pecans

Preheat oven to 350°. In small saucepan, melt *1 cup* margarine; stir in *¼ cup* cocoa and *1 tablespoon* coffee, then water. Bring to a boil; remove from heat. In large mixer bowl, combine flour, brown sugar, baking soda, cinnamon and salt. Add cocoa mixture; mix well. Stir in *⅓ cup* sweetened condensed milk, eggs and vanilla. Pour into greased 15×10-inch jellyroll pan. Bake 15 minutes or until cake springs back when lightly touched. In small saucepan, melt remaining *¼ cup* margarine; stir in remaining *¼ cup* cocoa and *1 tablespoon* coffee. Add remaining sweetened condensed milk; stir in confectioners' sugar and nuts. Spread on warm cake.

ORANGE SPICE CAKE

Makes one 8-inch cake

1 (18¼- or 18½-ounce) package spice
    cake mix
1 (14-ounce) can Eagle® Brand
    Sweetened Condensed Milk
    (NOT evaporated milk)
1 (6-ounce) can frozen orange juice
    concentrate, thawed
2 teaspoons grated orange rind
1 (4-ounce) container frozen non-dairy
    whipped topping, thawed

Preheat oven to 350°. Prepare and bake cake mix as package directs for two 8- or 9-inch round layers. Remove from pans; cool thoroughly. Split layers. In medium mixing bowl, combine sweetened condensed milk, juice concentrate and rind; mix well. Fold in whipped topping. Chill at least 1 hour. Use about ⅔ cup orange mixture between each layer; use remainder to frost top and side. Chill thoroughly. Store in refrigerator.

CREAMY BAKED CHEESECAKE

Makes one 9-inch cheesecake

⅓ cup margarine or butter, melted
1¼ cups graham cracker crumbs
¼ cup sugar
2 (8-ounce) packages cream cheese, softened
1 (14-ounce) can Eagle® Brand Sweetened Condensed Milk (NOT evaporated milk)
3 eggs
¼ cup ReaLemon® Lemon Juice from Concentrate
1 (8-ounce) container sour cream

Preheat oven to 300°. Combine margarine, crumbs and sugar; press firmly on bottom of 9-inch springform pan. In large mixer bowl, beat cheese until fluffy. Gradually beat in sweetened condensed milk until smooth. Add eggs and ReaLemon; mix well. Pour into prepared pan. Bake 50 to 55 minutes or until cake springs back when lightly touched. Cool. Chill. Remove side of pan. Spread sour cream on cheesecake. Serve with Peach Melba Topping if desired. Refrigerate leftovers.

New York Style Cheesecake: Omit ReaLemon and sour cream. Preheat oven to 350°. Beat 4 (8-ounce) packages cream cheese until fluffy. Gradually add sweetened condensed milk; beat until smooth. Add ⅓ cup unsifted flour, 4 eggs and 1 tablespoon vanilla extract; mix well. Pour into prepared pan. Bake 1 hour or until lightly browned. Cool. Chill. Garnish.

PEACH MELBA TOPPING

Reserve ⅔ cup syrup drained from 1 (10-ounce) package thawed frozen red raspberries. In small saucepan, combine reserved syrup, ¼ cup red currant jelly and 1 tablespoon cornstarch. Cook and stir until slightly thickened and glossy. Cool. Stir in raspberries. Drain 1 (16-ounce) can peach slices; arrange on cake. Top with sauce.

BUTTERSCOTCH CHEESECAKE

Makes one 9-inch cheesecake

⅓ cup margarine or butter, melted
1½ cups graham cracker crumbs
⅓ cup firmly packed brown sugar
1 (14-ounce) can Eagle® Brand
   Sweetened Condensed Milk
   (NOT evaporated milk)
¾ cup cold water
1 (3⅝-ounce) package butterscotch
   pudding and pie filling mix
3 (8-ounce) packages cream cheese,
   softened
3 eggs
1 teaspoon vanilla extract
   Whipped cream
   Crushed hard butterscotch candy

Preheat oven to 375°. Combine margarine, crumbs and sugar; press firmly on bottom of 9-inch springform pan. In medium saucepan, combine sweetened condensed milk and water; mix well. Stir in pudding mix. Over medium heat, cook and stir until thickened and bubbly. In large mixer bowl, beat cheese until fluffy. Beat in eggs and vanilla then pudding mixture. Pour into prepared pan. Bake 50 minutes or until golden brown around edge (center will be soft). Cool to room temperature. Chill thoroughly. Garnish with whipped cream and crushed candy. Refrigerate leftovers.

CHEESELESS "CHEESECAKE"

Makes 9 servings

4 eggs, separated
1 (14-ounce) can Eagle® Brand
   Sweetened Condensed Milk
   (NOT evaporated milk)
3 tablespoons ReaLemon® Lemon Juice
   from Concentrate
1½ teaspoons cornstarch
12 slices zwieback toast, crushed (about
   1 cup)

Preheat oven to 350°. In medium mixing bowl, beat egg yolks. Add sweetened condensed milk, ReaLemon and cornstarch; mix well. In small mixer bowl, beat egg whites until stiff but not dry; fold into sweetened condensed milk mixture. Sprinkle half the zwieback crumbs into greased 9-inch square baking pan. Pour filling evenly over crumbs. Top with remaining crumbs. Bake 30 minutes or until wooden pick inserted near center comes out clean. Cool to room temperature. Chill thoroughly. Cut into squares to serve. Refrigerate leftovers.

Butterscotch Cheesecake

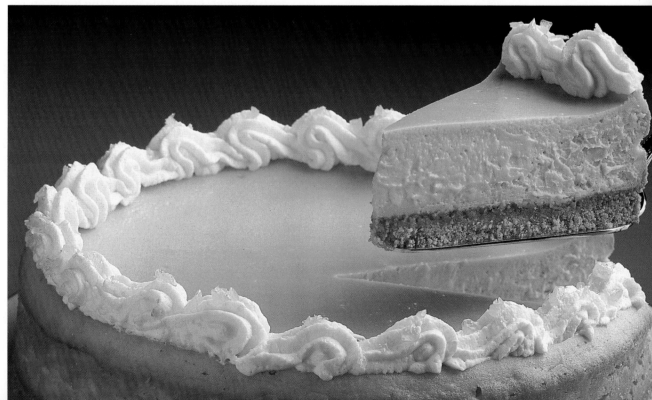

BLACK FOREST TORTE

Makes one 9-inch cake

1 (18¼- or 18½-ounce) package
    chocolate cake mix
1 (21-ounce) can cherry pie filling,
    drained and chilled, reserving
    ½ cup sauce
1 (6-ounce) package semi-sweet
    chocolate chips
1 (14-ounce) can Eagle® Brand
    Sweetened Condensed Milk
    (NOT evaporated milk)
½ teaspoon almond extract

Preheat oven to 350°. Prepare and bake cake mix as package directs for two 9-inch round layers. Remove from pans; cool thoroughly. In heavy saucepan, over medium heat, melt chips with sweetened condensed milk. Cook and stir until mixture thickens, about 10 minutes. Cool 20 minutes. Meanwhile, combine cherries, reserved sauce and extract. Place 1 cake layer on serving plate, top side up. With sharp knife, remove crust from top of cake layer to within ½ inch of edge; top with half the chocolate mixture then the cherries. Top with second cake layer and remaining chocolate mixture. Garnish as desired.

PEANUT BUTTER FROSTING

Makes about 3½ cups

1 (8-ounce) package cream cheese,
    softened
1 (14-ounce) can Eagle® Brand
    Sweetened Condensed Milk
    (NOT evaporated milk)
1 cup peanut butter

In small mixer bowl, beat cheese until fluffy. Gradually beat in sweetened condensed milk then peanut butter until smooth. Use to frost one (8- or 9-inch) two-layer cake or 4 dozen cupcakes or one (15×10-inch) sheet cake. Refrigerate leftovers.

CHOCOLATE COCONUT PECAN TORTE

Makes one 8- or 9-inch cake

1 (18¼- or 18½-ounce) package
    chocolate cake mix
1 (14-ounce) can Eagle® Brand
    Sweetened Condensed Milk
    (NOT evaporated milk)
3 egg yolks, beaten
½ cup margarine or butter
1 (3½-ounce) can flaked coconut
    (1⅓ cups)
1 cup chopped pecans
1 teaspoon vanilla extract
2 cups frozen non-dairy whipped
    topping, thawed or 1 cup (½ pint)
    whipping cream, whipped
Pecan halves, optional

Preheat oven to 350°. Prepare cake mix as package directs. Pour batter into three well-greased and floured 8- or 9-inch round layer cake pans. Bake 20 minutes or until wooden pick inserted near center comes out clean. Remove from pans; cool thoroughly. Meanwhile, in heavy saucepan, combine sweetened condensed milk, egg yolks and margarine. Over medium heat, cook and stir until thickened or bubbly, about 10 minutes. Stir in coconut, pecans and vanilla. Cool 10 minutes. With sharp knife, remove crust from top of each cake layer to within ½ inch of edge. Spread equal portions of coconut pecan mixture between layers and on top to within ½ inch of edge. Frost side and ½-inch rim on top of cake with whipped topping. Garnish with pecan halves if desired. Store cake in refrigerator.

Black Forest Torte (top)
Chocolate Coconut Pecan Torte (bottom)

CREAMY FRUIT 'N' NUT ▲ CHEESECAKE

Makes one 9-inch cheesecake

⅓ cup margarine or butter, melted
1¼ cups graham cracker crumbs
¼ cup sugar
2 (8-ounce) packages cream cheese, softened
1 (14-ounce) can Eagle® Brand Sweetened Condensed Milk (NOT evaporated milk)
1 envelope unflavored gelatine
¼ cup ReaLemon® Lemon Juice from Concentrate
1⅓ cups (one-half 28-ounce jar) None Such® Ready-to-Use Mincemeat
½ cup chopped nuts
1 tablespoon grated lemon rind
1 cup (½ pint) whipping cream, whipped
Sour cream and additional nuts, optional

Combine margarine, crumbs and sugar; press firmly on bottom of 9-inch springform pan. In large mixer bowl, beat cheese until fluffy. Gradually beat in sweetened condensed milk until smooth. In small saucepan, sprinkle gelatine over ReaLemon; let stand 1 minute. Over low heat, stir until gelatine dissolves. Add to cheese mixture with mincemeat, nuts and rind; mix well. Fold in whipped cream; pour into prepared pan. Chill 3 hours or until set. Garnish with sour cream and additional nuts if desired. Refrigerate leftovers.

AMBROSIA COMPANY CAKE

Makes 12 to 15 servings

1 (18¼- or 18½-ounce) package yellow or white cake mix
1 (14-ounce) can Eagle® Brand Sweetened Condensed Milk (NOT evaporated milk)
2 tablespoons frozen orange juice concentrate, thawed
1 teaspoon grated orange rind
1 (4-ounce) container frozen non-dairy whipped topping, thawed
⅓ cup flaked coconut, toasted
Orange slices, optional

Preheat oven to 350°. Prepare and bake cake as package directs for 13×9-inch cake. Cool thoroughly. With table knife handle, poke holes about 1 inch apart in cake halfway through to bottom. Combine sweetened condensed milk, juice concentrate and rind; mix well. Spoon small amounts of mixture into each hole in cake; spread remaining mixture evenly over top. Chill at least 1 hour. Spread whipped topping over cake; garnish with coconut and orange slices if desired. Store in refrigerator.

STRAWBERRY TUNNEL CREAM CAKE

Makes one 10-inch cake

- 1 (10-inch) prepared round angel food cake
- 2 (3-ounce) packages cream cheese, softened
- 1 (14-ounce) can Eagle® Brand Sweetened Condensed Milk (NOT evaporated milk)
- ⅓ cup ReaLemon® Lemon Juice from Concentrate
- 1 teaspoon almond extract
- 2 to 4 drops red food coloring, optional
- 1 cup chopped fresh strawberries
- 1 (12-ounce) container frozen non-dairy whipped topping, thawed (5¼ cups)
- Additional fresh strawberries, optional

Invert cake onto serving plate. Cut 1-inch slice crosswise from top of cake; set aside. With sharp knife, cut around cake 1 inch from center hole and 1 inch from outer edge, leaving cake walls 1-inch thick. Remove cake from center, leaving 1-inch thick base on bottom of cake. Reserve cake pieces. In large mixer bowl, beat cheese until fluffy. Gradually beat in sweetened condensed milk until smooth. Stir in ReaLemon, extract and food coloring if desired. Stir in reserved torn cake pieces and chopped strawberries. Fold in *1 cup* whipped topping. Fill cavity of cake with strawberry mixture; replace top slice of cake. Chill 3 hours or until set. Frost with remaining whipped topping; garnish with strawberries if desired. Store in refrigerator.

CHOCOLATE CHIP CHEESECAKE

Makes one 9-inch cheesecake

1½ cups finely crushed creme-filled chocolate sandwich cookies (about 18 cookies)

2 to 3 tablespoons margarine or butter, melted

3 (8-ounce) packages cream cheese, softened

1 (14-ounce) can Eagle® Brand Sweetened Condensed Milk (NOT evaporated milk)

3 eggs

2 teaspoons vanilla extract

1 cup mini chocolate chips

1 teaspoon flour

Preheat oven to 300°. Combine cookie crumbs and margarine; press firmly on bottom of 9-inch springform pan. In large mixer bowl, beat cheese until fluffy. Gradually beat in sweetened condensed milk until smooth. Add eggs and vanilla; mix well. In small bowl, toss ½ cup chips with flour to coat; stir into cheese mixture. Pour into prepared pan. Sprinkle remaining ½ cup chips evenly over top. Bake 1 hour or until cake springs back when lightly touched. Cool to room temperature. Chill thoroughly. Garnish as desired. Refrigerate leftovers.

Tip: For best distribution of chips throughout cheesecake, do not oversoften or overbeat cream cheese.

Luscious Baked Chocolate Cheesecake (top), Chocolate Chip Cheesecake (bottom)

LUSCIOUS BAKED CHOCOLATE CHEESECAKE

Makes one 9-inch cheesecake

⅓ cup margarine or butter, melted
1¼ cups graham cracker crumbs
¼ cup sugar
  3 (8-ounce) packages cream cheese, softened
  1 (14-ounce) can Eagle® Brand Sweetened Condensed Milk (NOT evaporated milk)
  1 (12-ounce) package semi-sweet chocolate chips *or* 8 (1-ounce) squares semi-sweet chocolate, melted
  4 eggs
  2 teaspoons vanilla extract

Preheat oven to 300°. Combine margarine, crumbs and sugar; press on bottom of 9-inch springform pan. In large mixer bowl, beat cheese until fluffy. Gradually beat in sweetened condensed milk until smooth. Add remaining ingredients; mix well. Pour into prepared pan. Bake 1 hour and 5 minutes or until cake springs back when lightly touched. Cool to room temperature. Chill thoroughly. Garnish as desired. Refrigerate leftovers.

PEACH CREAM CAKE   ▲

Makes 10 to 12 servings

  1 (7-inch) prepared loaf angel food cake, frozen
  1 (14-ounce) can Eagle® Brand Sweetened Condensed Milk (NOT evaporated milk)
  1 cup cold water
  1 (3½-ounce) package instant vanilla pudding and pie filling mix
  1 teaspoon almond extract
  2 cups (1 pint) whipping cream, whipped
  4 cups sliced, pared fresh peaches *or*
  1 (20-ounce) package frozen sliced peaches, thawed

Cut cake into ¼-inch slices; arrange half the slices on bottom of 13×9-inch baking dish. In large mixer bowl, combine sweetened condensed milk and water; mix well. Add pudding mix; beat until well blended. Chill 5 minutes. Stir in extract; fold in whipped cream. Pour half the cream mixture over cake slices; arrange half the peach slices on top. Repeat layering, ending with peach slices. Chill 4 hours or until set. Cut into squares to serve. Refrigerate leftovers.

LEMON ANGEL ROLL

Makes 8 to 10 servings

- 1 (14½- or 16-ounce) package angel food cake mix
- 1 (14-ounce) can Eagle® Brand Sweetened Condensed Milk (NOT evaporated milk)
- ⅓ cup ReaLemon® Lemon Juice from Concentrate
- 2 teaspoons grated lemon rind
- 4 to 6 drops yellow food coloring, optional
- 1 (4-ounce) container frozen non-dairy whipped topping, thawed
- ½ cup flaked coconut, tinted yellow* if desired

Preheat oven to 350°. Line 15×10-inch jellyroll pan with aluminum foil, extending foil 1 inch over ends of pan. Prepare cake mix as package directs. Spread batter evenly into prepared pan. Bake 30 minutes or until top springs back when lightly touched. *Immediately* turn onto towel sprinkled with confectioners' sugar. Peel off foil; beginning at narrow end, roll up cake with towel, jellyroll-fashion. Cool thoroughly. Meanwhile, in medium mixing bowl, combine sweetened condensed milk, ReaLemon, rind and food coloring if desired; mix well. Fold in whipped topping. Unroll cake; trim edges. Spread with half the lemon filling; reroll. Place on serving plate, seam-side down; spread remaining filling over roll. Garnish with coconut. Chill thoroughly before serving. Store in refrigerator.

*To tint coconut: Combine coconut, ½ teaspoon water and 2 drops yellow food coloring in small plastic bag or bowl; shake or mix well.

Lemon Angel Roll Variations:

Chocolate Pecan Filling

½ cup margarine or butter
1 (1-ounce) square unsweetened
    chocolate
1 (14-ounce) can Eagle® Brand
    Sweetened Condensed Milk
    (NOT evaporated milk)
1 (3½-ounce) can flaked coconut
    (1⅓ cups)
¾ cup finely chopped pecans
1 teaspoon vanilla extract

Prepare cake roll as above. In medium
saucepan, melt margarine and chocolate with
sweetened condensed milk. Over medium heat,
cook and stir until mixture thickens, about 10
minutes. Add coconut, nuts and vanilla.
Spread all filling on cake; proceed as above.
Sprinkle with confectioners' sugar. Store
covered at room temperature or in refrigerator.

Cranberry Filling

1 cup fresh *or* dry-pack frozen
    cranberries
½ cup sugar
¼ cup water
1 (3-ounce) package cream cheese,
    softened
1 (14-ounce) can Eagle® Brand
    Sweetened Condensed Milk
    (NOT evaporated milk)
¼ cup ReaLemon® Lemon Juice from
    Concentrate
    Few drops red food coloring, optional

Prepare cake roll as above. In small saucepan,
combine cranberries, sugar and water. Bring
to a boil; reduce heat and simmer uncovered 5
to 7 minutes. *Drain* cranberries; puree in
blender. Cool. In small mixer bowl, beat cheese
until fluffy. Gradually beat in sweetened
condensed milk and ReaLemon until smooth.
Stir in cranberries and food coloring if desired.
Chill 1 hour. Reserving 1½ cups mixture for
outside, spread remaining filling on cake;
proceed as above.

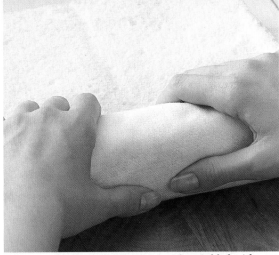

1. Invert cake *immediately* onto towel sprinkled with
confectioners' sugar. Peel off foil. Roll up cake with
towel; cool.

2. Unroll cooled cake. With serrated knife, trim uneven
crust edges. Spread with filling.

3. Carefully roll cake and filling. Place on serving plate,
seam-side down.

LEMON PARTY CHEESECAKE

Makes 15 servings

1 (18¼- or 18½-ounce) package yellow
   cake mix*
4 eggs
¼ cup vegetable oil
2 (8-ounce) packages cream cheese,
   softened
1 (14-ounce) can Eagle® Brand
   Sweetened Condensed Milk
   (NOT evaporated milk)
¼ to ⅓ cup ReaLemon® Lemon Juice
   from Concentrate
2 teaspoons grated lemon rind
1 teaspoon vanilla extract

Preheat oven to 300°. Reserve ½ *cup* dry cake
mix. In large mixer bowl, combine remaining
cake mix, *1 egg* and oil; mix well (mixture will
be crumbly). Press firmly on bottom and 1½
inches up sides of greased 13×9-inch baking
dish. In same bowl, beat cheese until fluffy.
Gradually beat in sweetened condensed milk
until smooth. Add remaining *3 eggs* and
reserved *½ cup* cake mix; on medium speed,
beat 1 minute. Stir in remaining ingredients.
Pour into prepared pan. Bake 50 to 55 minutes
or until center is firm. Cool to room
temperature. Chill thoroughly. Cut into
squares to serve. Garnish as desired.
Refrigerate leftovers.

*If "pudding added" cake mix is used, decrease
oil to 3 tablespoons.

NO-BAKE PEACH CHEESECAKE

Makes one 9-inch cheesecake

⅓ cup margarine or butter, melted
1¼ cups graham cracker crumbs
¼ cup sugar
1 (29-ounce) can peach halves, drained,
   reserving syrup
1 envelope unflavored gelatine
2 (8-ounce) packages cream cheese,
   softened
1 (14-ounce) can Eagle® Brand
   Sweetened Condensed Milk
   (NOT evaporated milk)
2 tablespoons ReaLemon® Lemon Juice
   from Concentrate
1 (4-ounce) container frozen non-dairy
   whipped topping, thawed

Combine margarine, crumbs and sugar.
Reserving 2 tablespoons for garnish, press
remaining crumbs firmly on bottom of 9-inch
springform pan or 13×9-inch baking pan. In
small saucepan, sprinkle gelatine over ½ *cup*
reserved syrup; let stand 1 minute. Over low
heat, stir until gelatine dissolves. Slice 2 peach
halves for garnish; reserve. In blender
container, blend remaining peaches until
smooth; combine with gelatine mixture and set
aside. In large mixer bowl, beat cheese until
fluffy; gradually beat in sweetened condensed
milk until smooth. Stir in ReaLemon and
peach mixture. Fold in whipped topping; turn
into prepared pan. Chill 3 hours or until set.
Garnish with peach slices. Refrigerate
leftovers.

Lemon Party Cheesecake

Fruitcake Bars (left), Fruitcake-in-a-Can (center), Chocolate Fruitcake (right)

EVER-SO-EASY FRUITCAKE

Makes one 10-inch cake

2½ cups unsifted flour
1 teaspoon baking soda
2 eggs, slightly beaten
1 (28-ounce) jar None Such® Ready-to-Use Mincemeat (Regular *or* Brandy and Rum)
1 (14-ounce) can Eagle® Brand Sweetened Condensed Milk (NOT evaporated milk)
2 cups (1 pound) mixed candied fruit
1 cup coarsely chopped nuts

Preheat oven to 300° Grease and flour 10-inch bundt pan. Combine flour and baking soda; set aside. In large bowl, combine remaining ingredients; blend in dry ingredients. Pour batter into prepared pan. Bake 1 hour and 45 to 50 minutes or until wooden pick comes out clean. Cool 15 minutes. Turn out of pan. Garnish as desired.

Fruitcake Bars: Grease 15×10-inch jellyroll pan; spread batter evenly in pan. Bake 40 to 45 minutes. Cool. Glaze if desired. Makes about 4 dozen bars.

Fruitcake-in-a-Can: Grease three 1-pound coffee cans; fill each can with about 2⅔ cups batter. Bake 1 hour and 20 to 25 minutes.

Chocolate Fruitcake: Prepare fruitcake batter as above, adding 3 (1-ounce) squares unsweetened chocolate, melted. For glaze, melt 3 (1-ounce) squares semi-sweet chocolate with 2 tablespoons margarine or butter. Spoon over fruitcake.

Fruitcake Cookies: Drop by rounded tablespoonfuls, 2 inches apart onto greased baking sheets. Bake 15 to 18 minutes. Makes about 5½ dozen cookies.

Fruitcake Loaves: Grease two 9×5-inch loaf pans; pour half the batter into each prepared pan. Bake 1 hour and 20 to 25 minutes.

Tip: To substitute condensed mincemeat for ready-to-use mincemeat, crumble 2 (9-ounce) packages None Such® Condensed Mincemeat into small saucepan; add 1½ cups water. Boil briskly 1 minute. Cool. Proceed as above.

COOKIES & COOKIE BARS

Try make-in-one-pan Magic Cookie Bars, nothing's easier! With Eagle Brand, stir up a batch of peanut butter cookies or chewy macaroons in minutes. There's a bar cookie or brownie here for every taste, every occasion. Looking for a special party cookie for the kids? Bake a batch of Versatile Cut-Out Cookies.

MACAROON ALMOND CRUMB BARS

Makes 36 bars

- 1 (18¼- or 18½-ounce) package chocolate cake mix
- ¼ cup vegetable oil
- 2 eggs
- 1 (14-ounce) can Eagle® Brand Sweetened Condensed Milk (NOT evaporated milk)
- ½ to 1 teaspoon almond extract
- 1½ cups coconut macaroon crumbs (about 8 macaroons)
- 1 cup chopped slivered almonds

Preheat oven to 350° (325° for glass dish). In large mixer bowl, combine cake mix, oil and *1 egg*. Beat on medium speed until crumbly. Press firmly on bottom of greased 13×9-inch baking pan. In medium mixing bowl, combine sweetened condensed milk, remaining egg and extract; mix well. Add *1 cup* macaroon crumbs and almonds. Spread evenly over prepared crust. Sprinkle with remaining *½ cup* crumbs. Bake 30 to 35 minutes or until lightly browned. Cool thoroughly. Cut into bars. Store loosely covered at room temperature.

TOFFEE BARS

Makes 36 bars

- ½ cup margarine or butter
- 1 cup oats
- ½ cup firmly packed brown sugar
- ½ cup unsifted flour
- ½ cup finely chopped walnuts
- ¼ teaspoon baking soda
- 1 (14-ounce) can Eagle® Brand Sweetened Condensed Milk (NOT evaporated milk)
- 2 teaspoons vanilla extract
- 1 (6-ounce) package semi-sweet chocolate chips

Preheat oven to 350°. In medium saucepan, melt *6 tablespoons* margarine; stir in oats, sugar, flour, nuts and baking soda. Press firmly on bottom of greased 13×9-inch baking pan; bake 10 to 15 minutes or until lightly browned. Meanwhile, in medium saucepan, combine remaining *2 tablespoons* margarine and sweetened condensed milk. Over medium heat, cook and stir until mixture thickens slightly, about 15 minutes. Remove from heat; stir in vanilla. Pour over crust. Return to oven; bake 10 to 15 minutes longer or until golden brown. Remove from oven; immediately sprinkle chips on top. Let stand 1 minute; spread while still warm. Cool to room temperature; chill thoroughly. Cut into bars. Store tightly covered at room temperature.

Top to Bottom: Double Chocolate Fantasy Bars (see page 39), Macaroon Almond Crumb Bars, Toffee Bars

EASY PEANUT BUTTER ▲ COOKIES

Makes about 5 dozen

1 (14-ounce) can Eagle® Brand
    Sweetened Condensed Milk
    (NOT evaporated milk)
¾ cup peanut butter
2 cups biscuit baking mix
1 teaspoon vanilla extract
    Granulated sugar

Preheat oven to 375°. In large mixer bowl, beat sweetened condensed milk and peanut butter until smooth. Add biscuit mix and vanilla; mix well. Shape into 1-inch balls. Roll in sugar. Place 2 inches apart on ungreased baking sheets. Flatten with fork. Bake 6 to 8 minutes or until *lightly* browned (do not overbake). Cool. Store tightly covered at room temperature.

Peanut Blossoms: Shape as above; *do not flatten*. Bake as above. Press milk chocolate candy kiss in center of each ball immediately after baking.

Peanut Butter & Jelly Gems: Press thumb in center of each ball of dough; fill with jelly, jam or preserves. Bake as above.

Any-Way-You-Like'm Cookies: Stir *1 cup* semi-sweet chocolate chips *or* chopped peanuts *or* raisins *or* flaked coconut into dough. Proceed as above.

◄CHOCO-COCONUT LAYER BARS

Makes 24 bars

⅓ cup margarine or butter, melted
¾ cup unsifted flour
½ cup sugar
2 tablespoons unsweetened cocoa
1 egg
1 (14-ounce) can Eagle® Brand
    Sweetened Condensed Milk
    (NOT evaporated milk)
1 (3½-ounce) can flaked coconut
    (1⅓ cups)
    Flavor Variations*
1 (6-ounce) package semi-sweet
    chocolate chips

Preheat oven to 350° (325° for glass dish). In medium mixing bowl, combine margarine, flour, sugar, cocoa and egg; mix well. Spread evenly into lightly greased 9-inch square baking pan. In small bowl, combine ¾ *cup* sweetened condensed milk, coconut and desired flavor variation; spread over chocolate layer. Bake 20 minutes or until lightly browned around edges. In heavy saucepan, over low heat, melt chips with remaining sweetened condensed milk. Remove from heat; spread evenly over coconut layer. Cool. Chill thoroughly. Cut into bars. Store loosely covered at room temperature.

*Flavor Variations:

Almond

  1 cup chopped slivered almonds
  ½ teaspoon almond extract

Mint

  ½ teaspoon peppermint extract
  4 drops green food coloring, optional

Cherry

  2 (6-ounce) jars maraschino cherries,
    chopped and well drained on paper
    towels

DOUBLE CHOCOLATE FANTASY BARS

Makes 36 bars

1 (18¼- or 18½-ounce) package
    chocolate cake mix
¼ cup vegetable oil
1 egg
1 cup chopped nuts
1 (14-ounce) can Eagle® Brand
    Sweetened Condensed Milk
    (NOT evaporated milk)
1 (6-ounce) package semi-sweet
    chocolate chips
1 teaspoon vanilla extract
    Dash salt

Preheat oven to 350°. In large mixer bowl, combine cake mix, oil and egg; beat on medium speed until crumbly. Stir in nuts. Reserving 1½ cups crumb mixture, press remainder on bottom of greased 13×9-inch baking pan. In small saucepan, combine remaining ingredients. Over medium heat, cook and stir until chips melt. Pour evenly over prepared crust. Sprinkle reserved crumb mixture evenly over top. Bake 25 to 30 minutes or until bubbly. Cool thoroughly. Cut into bars. Store loosely covered at room temperature.

PEANUTTY OAT BARS

Makes 36 bars

¼ cup margarine or butter
1½ cups quick-cooking oats
1 (3½-ounce) can flaked coconut
    (1⅓ cups)
1 (14-ounce) can Eagle® Brand
    Sweetened Condensed Milk
    (NOT evaporated milk)
1 cup peanut butter flavored chips
1 cup chopped nuts

Preheat oven to 350° (325° for glass dish). In 13×9-inch baking pan, melt margarine in oven. Sprinkle oats over margarine then coconut. Pour sweetened condensed milk evenly over top. Top evenly with chips then nuts; press down firmly. Bake 25 to 30 minutes or until lightly browned. Cool thoroughly. Cut into bars. Store loosely covered at room temperature.

MAGIC COOKIE BARS

Makes 36 bars

½ cup margarine or butter
1½ cups graham cracker *or* other
  crumbs*
1 (14-ounce) can Eagle® Brand
  Sweetened Condensed Milk
  (NOT evaporated milk)
1 cup semi-sweet chocolate chips *or*
  other toppings**
1 (3½-ounce) can flaked coconut
  (1⅓ cups)
1 cup chopped nuts***

Preheat oven to 350° (325° for glass dish). In 13×9-inch baking pan, melt margarine in oven. Sprinkle crumbs over margarine; pour sweetened condensed milk evenly over crumbs. Sprinkle with chips then coconut and nuts; press down firmly. Bake 25 to 30 minutes or until lightly browned. Cool. Chill thoroughly if desired. Cut into bars. Store loosely covered at room temperature.

*Crumbs

Vanilla wafer   Quick-cooking oats
Chocolate wafer   Wheat germ
Ginger snap cookie

**Toppings

Peanut butter flavored chips
Butterscotch flavored chips
Plain multi-colored candy-coated chocolate
  pieces
Raisins
Chopped dried apricots
Almond brickle chips
Banana chips
Chopped candied cherries
Small gumdrop candies
Miniature marshmallows

***Nuts

Walnuts	Almonds	Cashews
Pecans	Peanuts	Macadamia

Flavor Variations:

Mint: Combine ½ teaspoon peppermint extract and 4 drops green food coloring if desired with sweetened condensed milk. Proceed as above.

Mocha: Add 1 tablespoon instant coffee and 1 tablespoon chocolate flavored syrup with sweetened condensed milk. Proceed as above.

Peanut Butter: Combine ⅓ cup peanut butter with sweetened condensed milk. Proceed as above.

Maple: Combine ½ to 1 teaspoon maple flavoring with sweetened condensed milk. Proceed as above.

COCONUT MACAROONS

Makes about 4 dozen

2 (7-ounce) packages *flaked* coconut
    (5⅓ cups)
1 (14-ounce) can Eagle® Brand
    Sweetened Condensed Milk
    (NOT evaporated milk)
2 teaspoons vanilla extract
1½ teaspoons almond extract

Preheat oven to 350°. In large mixing bowl, combine coconut, sweetened condensed milk and extracts; mix well. Drop by rounded teaspoonfuls onto aluminum foil-lined and *generously greased* baking sheets; garnish as desired. Bake 8 to 10 minutes or until lightly browned around edges. *Immediately* remove from baking sheets (macaroons will stick if allowed to cool). Store loosely covered at room temperature.

Chocolate: Omit almond extract. Add 4 (1-ounce) squares unsweetened chocolate, melted. Proceed as above.

Chocolate Chip: Omit almond extract. Add 1 cup mini chocolate chips. Proceed as above.

Cherry Nut: Omit almond extract. Add 1 cup chopped nuts and 2 tablespoons maraschino cherry syrup. Press maraschino cherry half into center of each macaroon before baking.

Rum Raisin: Omit almond extract. Add 1 cup raisins and 1 teaspoon rum flavoring. Proceed as above.

Almond Brickle: Add ½ cup almond brickle chips. Proceed as above. Bake 10 to 12 minutes. Cool 3 minutes; remove from baking sheets.

Maple Walnut: Omit almond extract. Add ½ cup finely chopped walnuts and ½ teaspoon maple flavoring. Proceed as above.

Nutty Oat: Omit almond extract. Add 1 cup oats and 1 cup chopped nuts. Proceed as above.

Tip: To reduce cost, omit 1 (7-ounce) package coconut and substitute 2 cups fresh bread crumbs (4 slices bread).

CASHEW PEANUT BUTTER BARS

Makes 36 bars

- 1 cup unsifted flour
- ¼ cup firmly packed brown sugar
- ½ teaspoon baking powder
- ¼ teaspoon baking soda
- ½ cup cold margarine or butter, cut into small pieces
- 1 tablespoon vanilla extract
- 3 cups Campfire® Miniature Marshmallows
- 1 (14-ounce) can Eagle® Brand Sweetened Condensed Milk (NOT evaporated milk)
- 1 cup peanut butter flavored chips *or* ½ cup creamy peanut butter
- 1 (3-ounce) can chow mein noodles
- 1 cup coarsely chopped cashews *or* peanuts

Preheat oven to 350°. In medium mixing bowl, combine flour, sugar, baking powder and baking soda. Cut in margarine and *1 teaspoon* vanilla until mixture resembles coarse corn meal. Press firmly on bottom of ungreased 13×9-inch baking pan. Bake 15 minutes or until lightly browned. Top evenly with marshmallows; bake 2 minutes longer or until marshmallows begin to puff. Remove from oven; cool. Meanwhile, in heavy saucepan, over medium heat, combine sweetened condensed milk and peanut butter chips; cook and stir until slightly thickened, 6 to 8 minutes. Remove from heat; stir in remaining ingredients, including remaining vanilla. Spread evenly over marshmallows. Chill thoroughly. Cut into bars. Store loosely covered at room temperature.

Cashew Peanut Butter Bars

MILK CHOCOLATE BROWNIES

Makes 40 brownies

- 1 (12-ounce) package semi-sweet chocolate chips
- ¼ cup margarine or butter
- 2 cups biscuit baking mix
- 1 (14-ounce) can Eagle® Brand Sweetened Condensed Milk (NOT evaporated milk)
- 1 egg, beaten
- 1 teaspoon vanilla extract
- 1 cup chopped walnuts
  Confectioners' sugar

Preheat oven to 350°. In large saucepan, over low heat, melt *1 cup* chips with margarine; remove from heat. Add biscuit mix, sweetened condensed milk, egg and vanilla. Stir in nuts and remaining chips. Turn into well-greased 13×9-inch baking pan. Bake 20 to 25 minutes or until brownies begin to pull away from side of pan. Cool. Sprinkle with confectioners' sugar. Cut into squares. Store tightly covered at room temperature.

CHOCOLATE PEANUT BUTTER CHIP COOKIES

Makes about 4 dozen

- 8 (1-ounce) squares semi-sweet chocolate
- 3 tablespoons margarine or butter
- 1 (14-ounce) can Eagle® Brand Sweetened Condensed Milk (NOT evaporated milk)
- 2 cups biscuit baking mix
- 1 teaspoon vanilla extract
- 1 cup peanut butter flavored chips

Preheat oven to 350°. In large saucepan, over low heat, melt chocolate and margarine with sweetened condensed milk; remove from heat. Add biscuit mix and vanilla; with mixer, beat until smooth and well blended. Cool to room temperature. Stir in chips. Shape into 1¼-inch balls. Place 2 inches apart on ungreased baking sheets. Bake 6 to 8 minutes or until tops are slightly crusted. Cool. Store tightly covered at room temperature.

TRIPLE LAYER ▲
COOKIE BARS

Makes 36 bars

½ cup margarine or butter
1½ cups graham cracker crumbs
  1 (7-ounce) package flaked coconut
      (2⅔ cups)
  1 (14-ounce) can Eagle® Brand
      Sweetened Condensed Milk
      (NOT evaporated milk)
  1 (12-ounce) package semi-sweet
      chocolate chips
½ cup creamy peanut butter

Preheat oven to 350° (325° for glass dish). In 13×9-inch baking pan, melt margarine in oven. Sprinkle crumbs evenly over margarine. Top evenly with coconut then sweetened condensed milk. Bake 25 minutes or until lightly browned. In small saucepan, over low heat, melt chips with peanut butter. Spread evenly over hot coconut layer. Cool 30 minutes. Chill thoroughly. Cut into bars. Store loosely covered at room temperature.

PECAN PIE BARS ▲

Makes 36 bars

  2 cups unsifted flour
½ cup confectioners' sugar
  1 cup cold margarine or butter
  1 (14-ounce) can Eagle® Brand
      Sweetened Condensed Milk
      (NOT evaporated milk)
  1 egg
  1 teaspoon vanilla extract
  1 (6-ounce) package almond brickle
      chips
  1 cup chopped pecans

Preheat oven to 350° (325° for glass dish). In medium mixing bowl, combine flour and sugar; cut in margarine until mixture resembles coarse corn meal. Press firmly on bottom of 13×9-inch baking pan. Bake 15 minutes. Meanwhile, in medium mixing bowl, beat sweetened condensed milk, egg and vanilla. Stir in chips and pecans. Spread evenly over prepared crust. Bake 25 minutes or until golden brown. Cool. Chill thoroughly. Cut into bars. Store covered in refrigerator.

LAYERED LEMON CRUMB BARS

Makes 36 bars

1 (14-ounce) can Eagle® Brand Sweetened Condensed Milk (NOT evaporated milk)
½ cup ReaLemon® Lemon Juice from Concentrate
1 teaspoon grated lemon rind
⅔ cup margarine or butter, softened
1 cup firmly packed light brown sugar
1½ cups unsifted flour
1 cup oats
1 teaspoon baking powder
½ teaspoon salt
½ teaspoon ground cinnamon
½ teaspoon ground nutmeg

Preheat oven to 350° (325° for glass dish). In small mixing bowl, combine sweetened condensed milk, ReaLemon and rind; set aside. In large mixer bowl, beat margarine and sugar until fluffy; add flour, oats, baking powder and salt. Mix until crumbly. Spread half the oat mixture into lightly greased 13×9-inch baking pan. Press down firmly; spread lemon mixture evenly over crust. Stir spices into remaining crumb mixture; sprinkle evenly over lemon layer. Bake 20 to 25 minutes or until lightly browned. Chill thoroughly. Cut into bars. Store covered in refrigerator.

DOUBLE PEANUT-CHOCO BARS

Makes 36 bars

1 (18¼- or 18½-ounce) package white cake mix
½ cup plus ⅓ cup peanut butter
1 egg
1 (14-ounce) can Eagle® Brand Sweetened Condensed Milk (NOT evaporated milk)
1 (6-ounce) package semi-sweet chocolate chips
¾ cup Spanish peanuts

Top to Bottom: Double Peanut-Choco Bars, Chocolate Mint Bars, Layered Lemon Crumb Bars

Preheat oven to 350° (325° for glass dish). In large mixer bowl, combine cake mix, ½ cup peanut butter and egg; beat on low speed until crumbly. Press firmly on bottom of greased 13×9-inch baking pan. In medium mixing bowl, combine sweetened condensed milk and remaining ⅓ cup peanut butter; mix well. Spread evenly over prepared crust. Top with chips and peanuts. Bake 30 to 35 minutes or until lightly browned. Cool thoroughly. Cut into bars. Store loosely covered at room temperature.

CHOCOLATE MINT BARS

Makes 48 bars

1 (6-ounce) package semi-sweet chocolate chips
1 (14-ounce) can Eagle® Brand Sweetened Condensed Milk (NOT evaporated milk)
¾ cup plus 2 tablespoons margarine or butter
½ teaspoon peppermint extract
1¼ cups firmly packed light brown sugar
1 egg
1½ cups unsifted flour
1½ cups quick-cooking oats
¾ cup chopped nuts
⅓ cup crushed hard peppermint candy, optional

Preheat oven to 350°. In heavy saucepan, over low heat, melt chips with sweetened condensed milk and *2 tablespoons* margarine; remove from heat. Add extract; set aside. In large mixer bowl, beat remaining *¾ cup* margarine and sugar until fluffy; beat in egg. Add flour and oats; mix well. With floured hands, press two-thirds oat mixture into greased 15×10-inch jellyroll pan; spread chocolate mixture evenly on top. Add nuts to remaining oat mixture; crumble evenly over chocolate. Sprinkle with peppermint candy if desired. Bake 15 to 18 minutes or until edges are lightly browned. Cool thoroughly. Cut into bars. Store loosely covered at room temperature.

GERMAN CHOCOLATE SNACKIN' BARS ▲

Makes 36 bars

1 (4-ounce) package sweet cooking chocolate
¼ cup margarine or butter
1 (14-ounce) can Eagle® Brand Sweetened Condensed Milk (NOT evaporated milk)
2 eggs
½ cup biscuit baking mix
1 teaspoon vanilla extract
1 (7-ounce) package flaked coconut (2⅔ cups)
1 cup chopped pecans

Preheat oven to 325°. In medium saucepan, over low heat, melt chocolate with margarine. Remove from heat; stir in ½ cup sweetened condensed milk, eggs, biscuit mix and vanilla. Spread evenly into greased 13×9-inch baking dish. In medium bowl, combine remaining sweetened condensed milk and coconut. Spoon in small amounts evenly over chocolate mixture. Sprinkle nuts over top; press down firmly. Bake 25 minutes or until wooden pick inserted near center comes out clean. Cool thoroughly. Cut into bars. Store loosely covered at room temperature.

VERSATILE CUT-OUT COOKIES

Makes about 6½ dozen

3 cups unsifted flour
1 tablespoon baking powder
½ teaspoon salt
1 (14-ounce) can Eagle® Brand Sweetened Condensed Milk (NOT evaporated milk)
¾ cup margarine or butter, softened
2 eggs
2 teaspoons vanilla *or* 1½ teaspoons almond *or* lemon extract
Ready-to-spread frosting

Preheat oven to 350°. Combine flour, baking powder and salt; set aside. In large mixer bowl, beat sweetened condensed milk, margarine, eggs and vanilla until well blended. Add dry ingredients; mix well. On floured surface, lightly knead dough to form a smooth ball. Divide into thirds. On well-floured surface, roll out each portion to ⅛-inch thickness. Cut with floured cookie cutter. Place 1 inch apart on greased baking sheets. Bake 7 to 9 minutes or until lightly browned around edges. Cool thoroughly. Frost and decorate as desired with ready-to-spread frosting. Store loosely covered at room temperature.

Sandwich Cookies: Use 2½-inch cookie cutter. Bake as directed. Sandwich 2 cookies together with ready-to-spread frosting. Sprinkle with sugar if desired. (Makes about 3 dozen)

MINI FRUITCAKE MORSELS

Makes about 7 dozen

½ cup unsifted flour
1 teaspoon baking soda
1 (28-ounce) jar None Such® Ready-to-Use Mincemeat
1 (14-ounce) can Eagle® Brand Sweetened Condensed Milk (NOT evaporated milk)
2 cups graham cracker crumbs
1 cup chopped nuts
3 eggs, beaten
   Red and green candied cherries, halved

Preheat oven to 300°. In large mixing bowl, combine flour and baking soda. Add remaining ingredients except cherries; mix well. Line 1¾-inch muffin cups with paper liners or grease lightly. Spoon 1 level measuring tablespoon batter into each cup. Top each with cherry half. Bake 25 to 30 minutes or until wooden pick inserted near center comes out clean. Cool. Store loosely covered at room temperature.

CHOCOLATE ALMOND BARS

Makes 24 bars

1 cup slivered almonds, toasted and chopped
¼ cup margarine or butter, melted
1 (14-ounce) can Eagle® Brand Sweetened Condensed Milk (NOT evaporated milk)
1¼ cups graham cracker crumbs
½ teaspoon almond extract
½ teaspoon ground cinnamon, optional
1 (6-ounce) package semi-sweet chocolate chips

Preheat oven to 350°. In large mixing bowl, combine all ingredients except ½ cup chocolate chips; mix well. Spread evenly into greased 12×7-inch baking dish. Bake 20 minutes or until golden brown. Remove from oven; immediately sprinkle remaining ½ cup chips over top. Let stand 1 minute; spread while still warm. Cool thoroughly. Cut into bars. Store loosely covered at room temperature.

DOUBLE CHOCOLATE CHERRY COOKIES ▲

Makes about 10 dozen

1¼ cups margarine or butter, softened
1¾ cups sugar
2 eggs
1 tablespoon vanilla extract
3½ cups unsifted flour
¾ cup unsweetened cocoa
½ teaspoon baking powder
½ teaspoon baking soda
¼ teaspoon salt
2 (6-ounce) jars maraschino cherries, well drained and halved (about 60 cherries)
1 (6-ounce) package semi-sweet chocolate chips
1 (14-ounce) can Eagle® Brand Sweetened Condensed Milk (NOT evaporated milk)

Preheat oven to 350°. In large mixer bowl, beat margarine and sugar until fluffy; add eggs and vanilla. Mix well. Combine dry ingredients; stir into margarine mixture (dough will be stiff). Shape into 1-inch balls. Place 1 inch apart on ungreased baking sheets. Press cherry half into center of each cookie. Bake 8 to 10 minutes. Cool. In heavy saucepan, over medium heat, melt chips with sweetened condensed milk; continue cooking about 3 minutes or until mixture thickens. Frost each cookie, covering cherry. Store loosely covered at room temperature.

Double Chocolate Pecan Cookies: Prepare cookies as directed omitting cherries; flatten. Bake as directed and frost tops. Garnish each cookie with pecan half.

APPLESAUCE FRUITCAKE BARS ▲

Makes 48 bars

1 (14-ounce) can Eagle® Brand
    Sweetened Condensed Milk
    (NOT evaporated milk)
2 eggs
¼ cup margarine or butter, melted
2 teaspoons vanilla extract
3 cups biscuit baking mix
1 (15-ounce) jar applesauce
1 cup chopped dates
1 (6-ounce) container green candied
    cherries, chopped
1 (6-ounce) container red candied
    cherries, chopped
1 cup chopped nuts
1 cup raisins
    Confectioners' sugar

Preheat oven to 325°. In large mixer bowl, beat sweetened condensed milk, eggs, margarine and vanilla. Stir in remaining ingredients except confectioners' sugar. Spread evenly into well-greased and floured 15×10-inch jellyroll pan. Bake 35 to 40 minutes or until wooden pick inserted in center comes out clean. Cool thoroughly. Sprinkle with confectioners' sugar. Cut into bars. Store tightly covered at room temperature.

QUICK FRUIT SNACK MUNCHIES

Makes about 5 dozen

1 (14-ounce) can Eagle® Brand
    Sweetened Condensed Milk
    (NOT evaporated milk)
2 cups finely chopped dried apricots or
    dates
¾ cup finely chopped nuts
1 teaspoon vanilla extract
1 (12-ounce) package butter- or
    cheese-flavored crackers

In heavy saucepan, over medium heat, combine sweetened condensed milk and apricots; cook and stir until thickened, about 8 minutes. Remove from heat; stir in nuts and vanilla. Spoon about 1 teaspoon mixture on cracker; top with another cracker. Repeat. Store covered at room temperature.

MICROWAVE: In 1-quart glass measure, combine sweetened condensed milk and apricots. Microwave on ½ power (medium) 5 to 6 minutes, stirring after 3 minutes. Stir in nuts and vanilla. Proceed as above.

BUTTERSCOTCH CHEESECAKE BARS

Makes 36 bars

1 (12-ounce) package butterscotch
    flavored chips
⅓ cup margarine or butter
2 cups graham cracker crumbs
1 cup chopped nuts
1 (8-ounce) package cream cheese,
    softened
1 (14-ounce) can Eagle® Brand
    Sweetened Condensed Milk
    (NOT evaporated milk)
1 egg
1 teaspoon vanilla extract

Preheat oven to 350° (325° for glass dish). In medium saucepan, melt chips and margarine; stir in crumbs and nuts. Press half the mixture firmly on bottom of greased 13×9-inch baking pan. In large mixer bowl, beat cheese until fluffy; gradually beat in sweetened condensed milk then egg and vanilla. Mix well. Pour into prepared pan; top evenly with remaining crumb mixture. Bake 25 to 30 minutes or until wooden pick inserted near center comes out clean. Cool. Chill thoroughly. Cut into bars. Store covered in refrigerator.

GRANOLA BARS

Makes 48 bars

3 cups oats
1 cup peanuts
1 cup raisins
1 cup sunflower meats
1½ teaspoons ground cinnamon
1 (14-ounce) can Eagle® Brand
    Sweetened Condensed Milk
    (NOT evaporated milk)
½ cup margarine or butter, melted

Preheat oven to 325°. Line 15×10-inch jellyroll pan with aluminum foil; grease. In large mixing bowl, combine all ingredients; mix well. Press evenly into prepared pan. Bake 25 to 30 minutes or until golden brown. Cool slightly; remove from pan and peel off foil. Cut into bars. Store loosely covered at room temperature.

MAKE-AHEAD S'MORES

Makes 32 servings

1 (8-ounce) package semi-sweet
    chocolate squares
1 (14-ounce) can Eagle® Brand
    Sweetened Condensed Milk
    (NOT evaporated milk)
1 teaspoon vanilla extract
32 (4¾×2⅛-inch) whole graham
    crackers
2 cups Campfire® Miniature
    Marshmallows

In heavy saucepan, over low heat, melt chocolate. Add sweetened condensed milk and vanilla; cook and stir until smooth. Making 1 sandwich at a time, spread 1 tablespoon chocolate mixture on each of 2 whole graham crackers; sprinkle 1 with marshmallows and gently press second graham cracker chocolate-side down on top. Repeat with remaining ingredients. Carefully break each sandwich in half before serving. Wrap with plastic wrap; store at room temperature.

MICROWAVE: In 1-quart glass measure, combine chocolate, sweetened condensed milk and vanilla. Microwave on full power (high) 2½ minutes. Stir until chocolate melts and mixture is smooth. Proceed as above.

Make-Ahead S'Mores

CLASSIC DESSERTS

Looking for that something special to complete the meal? Choose from these extra creamy puddings, custards and baked desserts. Top off ice cream with rich luscious Hot Fudge Sauce—try all the variations! And, Eagle Brand is the traditional ingredient in that classic Spanish dessert, Caramel Flan.

CARAMEL FLAN

Makes 10 to 12 servings

¾ cup sugar
4 eggs
1¾ cups water
1 (14-ounce) can Eagle® Brand
    Sweetened Condensed Milk
    (NOT evaporated milk)
½ teaspoon vanilla extract
⅛ teaspoon salt

Preheat oven to 350°. In heavy skillet, over medium heat, cook sugar, stirring constantly until melted and caramel-colored. Pour into ungreased 9-inch round layer cake pan, tilting to coat bottom completely. In medium mixing bowl, beat eggs; stir in water, sweetened condensed milk, vanilla and salt. Pour into caramelized pan; set in larger pan (a broiler pan). Fill larger pan with 1 inch hot water. Bake 55 to 60 minutes or until knife inserted near center comes out clean. Cool. Chill thoroughly. Loosen side of flan with knife; invert onto serving plate with rim. Garnish as desired. Refrigerate leftovers.

FRUIT GLAZED BAKED CUSTARDS

Makes 6 servings

3 eggs
1 (14-ounce) can Eagle® Brand
    Sweetened Condensed Milk
    (NOT evaporated milk)
1 cup water
1 teaspoon vanilla extract
½ cup red currant jelly
2 tablespoons orange-flavored liqueur
    or orange juice
1 tablespoon cornstarch
    Few drops red food coloring, optional
    Fresh strawberries or other fruit

Preheat oven to 350°. In medium mixing bowl, beat eggs; stir in sweetened condensed milk, water and vanilla. Pour equal portions of mixture into six 6-ounce custard cups. Set cups in shallow pan; fill pan with 1 inch hot water. Bake 45 to 50 minutes or until knife inserted in center comes out clean. Cool. In small saucepan, combine jelly, liqueur and cornstarch. Cook and stir until jelly melts and mixture comes to a boil. Stir in food coloring if desired. Cool to room temperature. Invert custards onto serving plates. Top with sauce and strawberries. Refrigerate leftovers.

Top to Bottom: Baked Almond Pudding (see page 53), Caramel Flan, Fruit Glazed Baked Custards

STRAWBERRIES & CREAM DESSERT

Makes 10 to 12 servings

1 (14-ounce) can Eagle® Brand
  Sweetened Condensed Milk
  (NOT evaporated milk)
1½ cups cold water
1 (3½-ounce) package instant vanilla
  pudding and pie filling mix
2 cups (1 pint) whipping cream,
  whipped
1 (12-ounce) prepared loaf pound cake,
  cut into cubes (about 6 cups)
4 cups sliced fresh strawberries
½ cup strawberry preserves
  Additional fresh strawberries
  Toasted slivered almonds

In large mixing bowl, combine sweetened condensed milk and water; mix well. Add pudding mix; beat until well blended. Chill 5 minutes. Fold in whipped cream. Spoon *2 cups* pudding mixture into 4-quart round glass serving bowl; top with half the cake cubes, half the strawberries, half the preserves and half the remaining pudding mixture. Repeat layering, ending with pudding mixture. Garnish with additional strawberries and almonds. Chill 4 hours or until set. Refrigerate leftovers.

BAKED ALMOND PUDDING

Makes 8 to 10 servings

¼ cup firmly packed brown sugar
¾ cup slivered almonds, toasted
1 (14-ounce) can Eagle® Brand Sweetened Condensed Milk (NOT evaporated milk)
5 eggs
1 cup (½ pint) whipping cream
½ teaspoon almond extract
Additional toasted almonds, optional

Preheat oven to 325°. In 8-inch round layer cake pan, sprinkle sugar; set aside. In blender or food processor container, grind nuts; add sweetened condensed milk, eggs, ½ cup cream and extract. Blend thoroughly. Pour into prepared pan; set in larger pan. Fill larger pan with 1 inch hot water. Bake 40 to 45 minutes or until knife inserted near center comes out clean. Cool. Chill thoroughly; invert onto serving plate. Beat remaining cream for garnish; top with additional almonds if desired. Refrigerate leftovers.

LIME CHIFFON SQUARES ▲

Makes 10 to 12 servings

¼ cup margarine or butter, melted
1 cup graham cracker crumbs
1 (3-ounce) package lime flavor gelatin
1 cup boiling water
1 (14-ounce) can Eagle® Brand Sweetened Condensed Milk (NOT evaporated milk)
1 (8-ounce) can crushed pineapple, undrained
2 tablespoons ReaLime® Lime Juice from Concentrate
4 cups Campfire® Miniature Marshmallows
1 cup (½ pint) whipping cream, whipped

Combine margarine and crumbs; press firmly on bottom of 9-inch square or 12×7-inch baking dish. In large mixing bowl, dissolve gelatin in water; stir in sweetened condensed milk, pineapple and ReaLime. Fold in marshmallows and whipped cream. Pour into prepared dish. Chill 2 hours or until set. Garnish as desired. Refrigerate leftovers.

BUTTERSCOTCH APPLE SQUARES ▲

Makes 12 servings

¼ cup margarine or butter
1½ cups graham cracker crumbs
2 small all-purpose apples, pared and chopped (about 1¼ cups)
1 (6-ounce) package butterscotch flavored chips
1 (14-ounce) can Eagle® Brand Sweetened Condensed Milk (NOT evaporated milk)
1 (3½-ounce) can flaked coconut (1⅓ cups)
1 cup chopped nuts

Preheat oven to 350° (325° for glass dish). In 3-quart shallow baking pan (13×9-inch), melt margarine in oven. Sprinkle crumbs evenly over margarine; top with apples. In heavy saucepan, over medium heat, melt chips with sweetened condensed milk. Pour butterscotch mixture evenly over apples. Top with coconut and nuts; press down firmly. Bake 25 to 30 minutes or until lightly browned. Cool. Chill thoroughly. Garnish as desired. Refrigerate leftovers.

MICROWAVE: In 2½-quart shallow baking dish (12×7-inch), microwave margarine on full power (high) 1 minute or until melted. Sprinkle crumbs evenly over margarine; top with apples. In 1-quart glass measure, microwave chips with sweetened condensed milk on ⅔ power (medium-high) 2 to 3 minutes. Mix well. Pour butterscotch mixture evenly over apples. Top with coconut and nuts. Press down firmly. Microwave on full power (high) 8 to 9 minutes. Proceed as above.

EASY LEMON PUDDING

Makes 6 to 8 servings

1 (14-ounce) can Eagle® Brand Sweetened Condensed Milk (NOT evaporated milk)
2½ cups cold water
2 (3¾-ounce) packages instant lemon pudding and pie filling mix

In large mixing bowl, combine sweetened condensed milk and water. Add pudding mix; beat until well blended. Chill thoroughly. Serve in individual dessert dishes or fill 12 medium-size cream puffs. Refrigerate leftovers.

CREAMY LEMON FROSTING

Makes about 2½ cups

1 (8-ounce) package cream cheese, softened
1 (14-ounce) can Eagle® Brand Sweetened Condensed Milk (NOT evaporated milk)
⅓ cup ReaLemon® Lemon Juice from Concentrate

In small mixer bowl, beat cheese until fluffy. Gradually beat in sweetened condensed milk until smooth. Stir in ReaLemon. Chill 1 hour. Use to frost one (13×9-inch) cake *or* one (15×10-inch) sheet cake *or* 2½ dozen cupcakes. Store in refrigerator.

CRUNCHY LEMON SQUARES

Makes 9 servings

1 cup unsifted flour
1 cup quick-cooking oats
½ cup coarsely chopped pecans
½ cup firmly packed light brown sugar
½ cup flaked coconut
1 teaspoon baking powder
½ cup margarine or butter, melted
1 (14-ounce) can Eagle® Brand Sweetened Condensed Milk (NOT evaporated milk)
½ cup ReaLemon® Lemon Juice from Concentrate
1 tablespoon grated lemon rind

Preheat oven to 350° (325° for glass dish). In medium mixing bowl, combine flour, oats, nuts, sugar, coconut, baking powder and margarine; stir until crumbly. Set aside. In medium mixing bowl, combine sweetened condensed milk, ReaLemon and rind. Press half the crumb mixture evenly on bottom of 9-inch square baking pan. Spread sweetened condensed milk mixture on top; sprinkle with remaining crumbs. Bake 25 to 30 minutes or until lightly browned. Cool. Chill thoroughly. Cut into squares; garnish as desired. Refrigerate leftovers.

CREAMY PECAN RUM SAUCE

Makes about 1½ cups

¼ cup margarine or butter
1 (14-ounce) can Eagle® Brand Sweetened Condensed Milk (NOT evaporated milk)
½ teaspoon rum flavoring
Dash salt
¼ cup chopped pecans

In small saucepan, over medium heat, melt margarine; add remaining ingredients. Cook and stir until slightly thickened, 10 to 12 minutes. Cool 10 minutes. *Sauce thickens as it cools.* Serve warm over baked apples, fruit or ice cream. Refrigerate leftovers.

MICROWAVE: In 1-quart glass measure, microwave margarine on full power (high) 1 minute or until melted. Stir in remaining ingredients. Microwave on ⅔ power (medium-high) 3 to 3½ minutes. Proceed as above.

To Reheat: In small heavy saucepan, combine desired amount of sauce with small amount of water. Over low heat, stir constantly until heated through.

Creamy Pecan Rum Sauce

FUDGY MILK CHOCOLATE FONDUE ▲

Makes about 3 cups

1 (16-ounce) can chocolate flavored
    syrup
1 (14-ounce) can Eagle® Brand
    Sweetened Condensed Milk
    (NOT evaporated milk)
    Dash salt
1½ teaspoons vanilla extract
    Dippers*

In heavy saucepan, combine syrup, sweetened condensed milk and salt. Over medium heat, cook and stir 12 to 15 minutes or until slightly thickened. Remove from heat; stir in vanilla. Serve warm with Dippers. Refrigerate leftovers.

*Dippers: pound cake cubes, melon balls, cherries with stems, pineapple chunks, orange slices, strawberries, banana slices, apple wedges, grapes, dried apricots, peach chunks, plum slices, pear slices, angel food cake cubes, kiwifruit slices and marshmallows.

MICROWAVE: In 1-quart glass measure, combine syrup, sweetened condensed milk and salt. Microwave on full power (high) 3½ to 4 minutes, stirring after 2 minutes. Stir in vanilla.

Tip: Can be served warm or cold over ice cream. Can be made several weeks ahead. Store tightly covered in refrigerator.

PUMPKIN RUM CUSTARDS

Makes 8 to 10 servings

1 cup sugar
4 eggs
1 (14-ounce) can Eagle® Brand
    Sweetened Condensed Milk
    (NOT evaporated milk)
1½ cups water
1 (16-ounce) can pumpkin (about
    2 cups)
⅓ cup light rum
½ teaspoon ground nutmeg
½ teaspoon salt
⅛ to ¼ teaspoon ground ginger

Preheat oven to 350°. In heavy skillet, over medium heat, cook sugar, stirring constantly until melted and caramel-colored. Using eight to ten 6-ounce custard cups, pour about 1 tablespoon caramelized sugar on bottom of each. In large mixer bowl, beat eggs; stir in remaining ingredients. Pour equal portions of mixture into prepared cups. Set cups in shallow pan; fill pan with 1 inch hot water. Bake 50 to 60 minutes or until knife inserted in center comes out clean. Cool. Chill thoroughly. Invert custards onto serving plates. Garnish as desired. Refrigerate leftovers.

SOUTHERN YAM DESSERT SQUARES ▶

Makes 8 to 10 servings

  2 cups quick-cooking oats
1½ cups unsifted flour
  ½ teaspoon baking soda
  ½ teaspoon salt
  1 cup margarine or butter, softened
  1 cup firmly packed light brown sugar
  1 teaspoon vanilla extract
  1 pound yams or sweet potatoes,
      cooked, peeled and mashed *or*
      1 (16- or 17-ounce) can yams,
      drained and mashed (about 2 cups)
  1 (14-ounce) can Eagle® Brand
      Sweetened Condensed Milk
      (NOT evaporated milk)
  2 eggs, beaten
1½ teaspoons ground allspice *or*
      pumpkin pie spice
  1 teaspoon grated orange rind
  ½ cup chopped nuts

Preheat oven to 350°. Combine oats, flour, baking soda and salt; set aside. In large mixer bowl, beat margarine, sugar and vanilla until fluffy. Add dry ingredients; mix until crumbly. Reserving *1 cup* crumb mixture, press remainder firmly on bottom of 13×9-inch baking dish. Bake 10 minutes. Meanwhile, in large mixing bowl, combine remaining ingredients except nuts; mix well. Pour over prepared crust. Combine nuts with reserved crumb mixture; crumble evenly over top. Bake 25 to 30 minutes or until golden brown. Cool. Serve warm or chilled. Garnish as desired. Refrigerate leftovers.

Tip: 1 (16-ounce) can pumpkin can be substituted for yams.

CREAMY DUTCH APPLE DESSERT

Makes 10 to 12 servings

  ¼ cup margarine or butter
1½ cups graham cracker crumbs
  1 (14-ounce) can Eagle® Brand
      Sweetened Condensed Milk
      (NOT evaporated milk)
  1 (8-ounce) container sour cream
  ¼ cup ReaLemon® Lemon Juice from
      Concentrate
  1 (21-ounce) can apple pie filling
  ¼ cup chopped walnuts
  ¼ teaspoon ground cinnamon

Preheat oven to 350°. In 1½-quart shallow baking dish (10×6-inch), melt margarine in oven. Sprinkle crumbs over margarine; mix well. Press firmly on bottom of dish. In medium mixing bowl, combine sweetened condensed milk, sour cream and ReaLemon; spread evenly over crumbs. Spoon pie filling evenly over creamy layer. Bake 25 to 30 minutes or until set. Cool slightly. Before serving, in small dish, stir together nuts and cinnamon; sprinkle over apple layer. Serve warm or chilled. Refrigerate leftovers.

CREAMY BANANA PUDDING

Makes 8 to 10 servings

- 1 (14-ounce) can Eagle® Brand Sweetened Condensed Milk (NOT evaporated milk)
- 1½ cups cold water
- 1 (3½-ounce) package instant vanilla pudding and pie filling mix
- 2 cups (1 pint) whipping cream, whipped
- 36 vanilla wafers
- 3 medium bananas, sliced and dipped in lemon juice

In large mixing bowl, combine sweetened condensed milk and water. Add pudding mix; beat until well blended. Chill 5 minutes. Fold in whipped cream. Spoon *1 cup* pudding mixture into 2½-quart round glass serving bowl. Top with one-third each of the vanilla wafers, bananas and pudding. Repeat layering twice, ending with pudding mixture. Chill thoroughly. Garnish as desired. Refrigerate leftovers.

Tip: Mixture can be layered in individual serving dishes.

CHERRY ALMOND CREAM DESSERT

Makes 10 to 12 servings

- 1 (14-ounce) can Eagle® Brand Sweetened Condensed Milk (NOT evaporated milk)
- 1½ cups cold water
- 1 (3½-ounce) package instant vanilla pudding and pie filling mix
- 1 teaspoon almond extract
- 2 cups (1 pint) whipping cream, whipped
- 1 (10¾- *or* 12-ounce) prepared loaf pound cake, cut into 10 slices
- 1 (21-ounce) can cherry pie filling, chilled
- Toasted almonds

In large mixing bowl, combine sweetened condensed milk and water. Add pudding mix and extract; beat until well blended. Chill 5 minutes. Fold in whipped cream. Spoon half the cream mixture into 13×9-inch baking dish; top with cake slices, pie filling, remaining cream mixture then almonds. Chill thoroughly. Refrigerate leftovers.

Creamy Banana Pudding

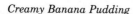

ORANGE NUT CREAM DESSERTS ▲

Makes 6 to 8 servings

1 (14-ounce) can Eagle® Brand
  Sweetened Condensed Milk
  (NOT evaporated milk)
1 (6-ounce) can frozen orange juice
  concentrate, thawed
1 (8-ounce) container sour cream
1 cup flaked coconut
½ cup chopped pecans
1 tablespoon grated orange rind
  Orange sections

In medium mixing bowl, combine sweetened
condensed milk and juice concentrate. Stir in
sour cream. In small bowl, combine coconut,
nuts and rind. Layer filling, coconut mixture
then orange sections in dessert dishes. Repeat,
ending with coconut mixture and orange
sections. Chill at least 2 hours. Refrigerate
leftovers.

STRAWBERRY CHIFFON SQUARES

Makes 12 servings

1½ cups vanilla wafer crumbs (about
  45 wafers)
⅓ cup margarine or butter, melted
1 (3-ounce) package strawberry flavor
  gelatin
¾ cup boiling water
1 (14-ounce) can Eagle® Brand
  Sweetened Condensed Milk
  (NOT evaporated milk)
1 (10-ounce) package frozen sliced
  strawberries in syrup, thawed
4 cups Campfire® Miniature
  Marshmallows
1 cup (½ pint) whipping cream,
  whipped

Combine crumbs and margarine; press firmly
on bottom of 12×7-inch baking dish. In large
mixing bowl, dissolve gelatin in water; stir in
sweetened condensed milk and undrained
strawberries. Fold in marshmallows and
whipped cream. Pour into prepared dish. Chill
2 hours or until set. Garnish as desired.
Refrigerate leftovers.

HOT FUDGE SAUCE

Makes about 1½ cups

1 (6-ounce) package semi-sweet
    chocolate chips *or* 4 (1-ounce)
    squares semi-sweet chocolate
2 tablespoons margarine or butter
1 (14-ounce) can Eagle® Brand
    Sweetened Condensed Milk
    (NOT evaporated milk)
  Dash salt
1 teaspoon vanilla extract

In heavy saucepan, over medium heat, melt
chips and margarine with sweetened
condensed milk and salt. Cook, stirring
constantly, until sauce is slightly thickened,
about 5 minutes. Remove from heat; stir in
vanilla. Serve warm over ice cream.
Refrigerate leftovers.

MICROWAVE: In 1-quart glass measure,
combine chips and margarine. Microwave on
full power (high) 1 minute; stir. Add remaining
ingredients; mix well. Microwave on full power
(high) 2 to 2½ minutes, stirring after each
minute.

To Reheat: In small heavy saucepan, combine
desired amount of sauce with small amount of
water. Over low heat, stir constantly until
heated through.

Variations

Mocha: Add 1 teaspoon instant coffee to chips
and margarine. Proceed as above.

Toasted Almond: Omit vanilla extract. Add
½ teaspoon almond extract. When sauce is
thickened, stir in ½ cup chopped toasted
almonds.

Choco-Mint: Omit vanilla extract. Add ½ to 1
teaspoon peppermint extract. Proceed as
above.

Spirited: Add ⅓ cup almond, coffee, mint *or*
orange-flavored liqueur after mixture has
thickened.

Mexican: Add 2 tablespoons coffee-flavored
liqueur *or* 1 teaspoon instant coffee dissolved
in 2 tablespoons water and 1 teaspoon ground
cinnamon after mixture has thickened.

*Top to Bottom: Peanut Butter Sauce, Hot Fudge Sauce,
Coconut Pecan Sauce*

PEANUT BUTTER SAUCE

Makes about 1½ cups

1 (14-ounce) can Eagle® Brand
Sweetened Condensed Milk
(NOT evaporated milk)
¼ to ⅓ cup peanut butter
Chopped peanuts, optional

In heavy saucepan, over low heat, combine
sweetened condensed milk and peanut butter;
cook and stir until well blended. Stir in nuts if
desired. Serve warm over ice cream.
Refrigerate leftovers.

MICROWAVE: In 1-quart glass measure,
combine sweetened condensed milk and
peanut butter. Microwave on full power (high)
2½ to 3½ minutes, stirring after each minute.
Proceed as above.

To Reheat: In small heavy saucepan, combine
desired amount of sauce with small amount of
water. Over low heat, stir constantly until
heated through.

COCONUT PECAN SAUCE

Makes about 2 cups

1 (14-ounce) can Eagle® Brand
Sweetened Condensed Milk
(NOT evaporated milk)
2 egg yolks, beaten
¼ cup margarine or butter
½ cup flaked coconut
½ cup chopped pecans
1 teaspoon vanilla extract

In heavy saucepan, combine sweetened
condensed milk, egg yolks and margarine.
Over medium heat, cook and stir until
thickened and bubbly, about 8 minutes. Stir in
remaining ingredients. Serve warm over ice
cream or cake.

MICROWAVE: In 1-quart glass measure,
combine sweetened condensed milk, egg yolks
and margarine. Microwave on ⅔ power
(medium-high) 3 minutes; stir. Microwave on
⅔ power (medium-high) 1 to 2 minutes.
Proceed as above.

To Reheat: In small heavy saucepan, combine
desired amount of sauce with small amount of
water. Over low heat, stir constantly until
heated through.

FLOATING ISLAND ▲
LIME DESSERTS

Makes 4 servings

Floating Islands*
1 (14-ounce) can Eagle® Brand
Sweetened Condensed Milk
(NOT evaporated milk)
2 egg yolks**
½ cup ReaLime® Lime Juice from
Concentrate
2 to 3 drops green food coloring,
optional
2 tablespoons flaked coconut, toasted

Prepare Floating Islands. Meanwhile, in
medium mixing bowl, beat sweetened
condensed milk and egg yolks; stir in ReaLime
and food coloring if desired. Spoon into four
6-ounce dessert dishes. Top each with a
Floating Island. Chill 2 hours or until set.
Garnish with coconut. Refrigerate leftovers.

***Floating Islands:** In small mixer bowl, beat
2 egg whites** until soft peaks form.
Gradually beat in 2 tablespoons sugar, beating
until stiff but not dry. Drop one-fourth of
mixture onto simmering water in large skillet;
repeat to make 4 islands. Simmer uncovered 5
minutes or until meringues are set. Remove
with slotted spoon; drain on paper towels.

****Use only Grade A clean, uncracked eggs.

GOLDEN BREAD PUDDING

Makes 6 to 8 servings

3 cups soft white bread cubes (4 slices
    bread)
3 eggs
3 cups warm water
1 (14-ounce) can Eagle® Brand
    Sweetened Condensed Milk
    (NOT evaporated milk)
2 tablespoons margarine or butter,
    melted
½ teaspoon salt
1 teaspoon vanilla extract

Preheat oven to 350°. Place bread cubes in
buttered 9-inch square baking pan. In large
mixing bowl, beat eggs; stir in remaining
ingredients. Pour evenly over bread cubes,
completely moistening bread. Bake 45 to 50
minutes or until knife inserted in center comes
out clean. Cool. Serve warm or chilled.
Refrigerate leftovers.

Tip: For firmer bread pudding, increase bread
cubes to 4 cups.

Apple Bread Pudding: Decrease water to 1¾
cups; increase margarine to ¼ cup and add 1
teaspoon ground cinnamon. In buttered 9-inch
square baking pan, combine 4 cups bread
cubes (5 slices bread), 2 cups pared, chopped
all-purpose apples (3 medium) and ½ cup
raisins. Proceed as above.

Pineapple Bread Pudding: Reduce water to
2¾ cups. Add 1 (8-ounce) can crushed
pineapple, undrained. Proceed as above.

Blueberry 'n' Spice Bread Pudding:
Reduce water to 1½ cups; increase margarine
to ¼ cup. Add 2 cups fresh *or* dry-pack frozen
blueberries to bread cubes. Add ½ teaspoon
ground cinnamon and ½ teaspoon ground
nutmeg. Proceed as above.

MAGIC-QUICK CHOCOLATE FROSTING

Makes about 1½ cups

2 (1-ounce) squares unsweetened
    chocolate
1 (14-ounce) can Eagle® Brand
    Sweetened Condensed Milk
    (NOT evaporated milk)
Dash salt
1 tablespoon water
½ teaspoon vanilla extract

In heavy saucepan, over medium heat, melt
chocolate with sweetened condensed milk and
salt. Cook and stir until mixture thickens,
about 10 minutes. Remove from heat. Stir in
water; cool. Stir in vanilla. Use to frost one (8-
or 9-inch) two-layer cake *or* one (13×9-inch)
cake. Store at room temperature.

MICROWAVE: In 1-quart glass measure,
combine chocolate, sweetened condensed milk
and salt. Microwave on full power (high) 3
minutes, stirring after 1½ minutes. Stir until
smooth. Proceed as above.

CREAMY RICE PUDDING

Makes 4 to 6 servings

2½ cups water
½ cup uncooked long grain rice
1 cinnamon stick *or* ¼ teaspoon ground
    cinnamon
2 (½-inch) pieces lemon rind
    Dash salt
1 (14-ounce) can Eagle® Brand
    Sweetened Condensed Milk
    (NOT evaporated milk)
    Additional ground cinnamon

In medium saucepan, combine water, rice,
cinnamon, lemon rind and salt; let stand 30
minutes. Bring to a boil, stirring occasionally.
Add sweetened condensed milk; mix well.
Return to a boil; stir. Reduce heat to medium.
Cook uncovered stirring frequently until liquid
is absorbed to top of rice, about 15 minutes.
Cool (pudding thickens as it cools). Remove
cinnamon stick and lemon rind. Sprinkle with
additional cinnamon. Serve warm or chilled.
Refrigerate leftovers.

RASPBERRY SWIRL DESSERT

Makes 10 to 12 servings

1 (7-ounce) package flaked coconut, toasted (2⅔ cups)
⅓ cup margarine or butter, melted
1 (10-ounce) package frozen red raspberries in syrup, thawed
1 tablespoon cornstarch
1 envelope unflavored gelatine
¼ cup water
1 (14-ounce) can Eagle® Brand Sweetened Condensed Milk (NOT evaporated milk)
1 (8-ounce) container sour cream
3 tablespoons orange-flavored liqueur
1 cup (½ pint) whipping cream, stiffly whipped

Combine coconut and margarine; press firmly on bottom and up side of 8- or 9-inch springform pan. Chill. In blender container, blend raspberries until smooth. In small saucepan, combine raspberries and cornstarch; cook and stir until mixture thickens. Cool to room temperature. Meanwhile, in small saucepan, sprinkle gelatine over water; let stand 1 minute. Over low heat, stir until gelatine dissolves; set aside. In large mixing bowl, combine sweetened condensed milk, sour cream, liqueur and gelatine; mix well. Fold in whipped cream. Chill 10 minutes or until mixture mounds slightly. Spread half the gelatine mixture into prepared pan; top with half the raspberry mixture in small amounts. Repeat layering. With metal spatula, swirl raspberry mixture through cream mixture. Chill 6 hours or until set. Garnish as desired. Refrigerate leftovers.

Raspberry Swirl Charlotte: Omit coconut and margarine. Line bottom and side of springform pan with 28 ladyfinger halves. Proceed as above.

ICE CREAM & FROZEN DESSERTS

With Eagle Brand, create super simple homemade ice creams—without an ice cream maker! Luscious make-ahead frozen pies and desserts like Peppermint Ice Cream Loaf are party perfect. Even elegant Grasshopper Baked Alaska is as easy as 1-2-3.

EASY HOMEMADE CHOCOLATE ICE CREAM

Makes about 1½ quarts

1 (14-ounce) can Eagle® Brand Sweetened Condensed Milk (NOT evaporated milk)
⅔ cup chocolate flavored syrup
2 cups (1 pint) whipping cream, whipped (*do not use non-dairy whipped topping*)

In large mixing bowl, combine sweetened condensed milk and syrup. Fold in whipped cream. Pour into 9×5-inch loaf pan or other 2-quart container; cover. Freeze 6 hours or until firm. Return leftovers to freezer.

Chocolate Mocha: Add 1 tablespoon instant coffee to sweetened condensed milk and syrup. Let stand 10 minutes. Proceed as above.

Chocolate Peanut Butter: Add ½ cup peanut butter. Proceed as above.

Chocolate Nut: Add ¾ cup chopped nuts. Proceed as above.

Chocolate Rocky Road: Add ½ cup chopped peanuts and 1 cup Campfire® Miniature Marshmallows. Proceed as above.

Chocolate Mint: Add 1 teaspoon peppermint extract. Proceed as above.

Chocolate Chocolate Chip: Add ¾ cup mini chocolate chips. Proceed as above.

Clockwise from Top: Easy Homemade French Vanilla Ice Cream (see page 66), Easy Homemade Chocolate Ice Cream, Peppermint Ice Cream Loaf

PEPPERMINT ICE CREAM LOAF

Makes 8 to 10 servings

2 cups finely crushed creme-filled chocolate sandwich cookies (about 20 cookies)
3 tablespoons margarine or butter, melted
1 cup crushed hard peppermint candy
¼ cup water
1 (14-ounce) can Eagle® Brand Sweetened Condensed Milk (NOT evaporated milk)
3 egg yolks*
1 to 2 drops red food coloring, optional
2 cups (1 pint) whipping cream, whipped (*do not use non-dairy whipped topping*)

Line 9×5-inch loaf pan with aluminum foil, extending foil above sides of pan. Combine crumbs and margarine; press firmly on bottom and halfway up sides of prepared pan. In blender container, blend *¼ cup* peppermint candy and water until candy dissolves. In large mixer bowl, beat sweetened condensed milk, egg yolks, food coloring if desired, *½ cup* crushed candy and peppermint liquid until well blended. Fold in whipped cream and remaining *¼ cup* crushed candy. Pour into prepared pan. Cover; freeze 6 hours or overnight. Remove from pan; peel off foil. To serve, garnish as desired and slice. Return leftovers to freezer.

*Use only Grade A clean, uncracked eggs.

FROZEN MOCHA CHEESECAKE ▲

Makes one 8- or 9-inch cheesecake

1¼ cups chocolate wafer cookie crumbs
    (about 24 wafers)
¼ cup margarine or butter, melted
¼ cup sugar
1 (8-ounce) package cream cheese,
    softened
1 (14-ounce) can Eagle® Brand
    Sweetened Condensed Milk
    (NOT evaporated milk)
⅔ cup chocolate flavored syrup
1 to 2 tablespoons instant coffee
1 teaspoon hot water
1 cup (½ pint) whipping cream,
    whipped
    Additional chocolate crumbs,
    optional

Combine crumbs, margarine and sugar; press firmly on bottom and up side of 8- or 9-inch springform pan or 13×9-inch baking pan. In large mixer bowl, beat cheese until fluffy. Gradually beat in sweetened condensed milk and chocolate syrup until smooth. In small bowl, dissolve coffee in water; add to cheese mixture. Mix well. Fold in whipped cream. Pour into prepared pan; cover. Freeze 6 hours or overnight. Garnish with chocolate crumbs if desired. Return leftovers to freezer.

EASY HOMEMADE FRENCH VANILLA ICE CREAM

Makes about 1½ quarts

1 (14-ounce) can Eagle® Brand
    Sweetened Condensed Milk
    (NOT evaporated milk)
3 eggs yolks,* beaten
4 teaspoons vanilla extract
2 cups (1 pint) whipping cream,
    whipped (do not use non-dairy
    whipped topping)

In large mixer bowl, beat sweetened condensed milk, egg yolks and vanilla until well blended. Fold in whipped cream. Pour into 9×5-inch loaf pan or other 2-quart container; cover. Freeze 6 hours or until firm. Return leftovers to freezer.

Vanilla Nut: Add ¾ cup chopped nuts. Proceed as above.

Coffee: Dissolve 1 tablespoon instant coffee in 1 teaspoon hot water; add to ice cream mixture. Proceed as above.

Chocolate Chip: Add ½ cup mini chocolate chips. Proceed as above.

Ice Cream 'n' Cookies: Fold in 1 cup coarsely crushed chocolate sandwich cookies. Proceed as above.

*Use only Grade A clean, uncracked eggs.

CHOCOLATE ICE CREAM CUPS

Makes about 1½ dozen

1 (12-ounce) package semi-sweet
  chocolate chips
1 (14-ounce) can Eagle® Brand
  Sweetened Condensed Milk
  (NOT evaporated milk)
1 cup finely ground pecans
  Ice cream, any flavor

In small saucepan, over low heat, melt chips
with sweetened condensed milk; remove from
heat. Stir in pecans. In individual paper-lined
muffin cups, spread about 2 tablespoons
chocolate mixture. With spoon, spread
chocolate on bottom and up side of each cup.
Freeze 2 hours or until firm. Before serving,
remove paper liners. Fill with ice cream. Store
unfilled cups tightly covered in freezer.

Use spoon to spread chocolate mixture to form cup.

FROZEN PASSION

Makes 2 to 3 quarts

2 (14-ounce) cans Eagle® Brand
  Sweetened Condensed Milk
  (NOT evaporated milk)
1 (2-liter) bottle *or* 2 (28-ounce) bottles
  or 5 (12-ounce) cans carbonated
  beverage, any flavor

Ice Cream Maker Method: In ice cream
freezer container, combine ingredients; mix
well. Freeze according to manufacturer's
instructions. Store leftovers in freezer.

Refrigerator-Freezer Method: In large
bowl, combine ingredients. Turn into
13×9-inch baking pan; freeze to a firm mush,
about 1 hour. Break into pieces and turn into
large mixer bowl. Beat until smooth. Return to
pan; cover. Freeze until firm.

Chocolate Cup with Orange Frozen Passion.

FROZEN PEANUT BUTTER PIE ▲

Makes one 9- or 10-inch pie

1 Chocolate Crunch Crust*
1 (8-ounce) package cream cheese, softened
1 (14-ounce) can Eagle® Brand Sweetened Condensed Milk (NOT evaporated milk)
¾ cup peanut butter
2 tablespoons ReaLemon® Lemon Juice from Concentrate
1 teaspoon vanilla extract
1 cup (½ pint) whipping cream, whipped or 1 (4-ounce) container frozen non-dairy whipped topping, thawed
  Chocolate fudge ice cream topping

In large mixer bowl, beat cheese until fluffy; gradually beat in sweetened condensed milk then peanut butter until smooth. Stir in ReaLemon and vanilla. Fold in whipped cream. Turn into prepared crust. Drizzle topping over pie. Freeze 4 hours or until firm. Return leftovers to freezer.

Chocolate Crunch Crust: In heavy saucepan, over low heat, melt ⅓ cup margarine or butter and 1 (6-ounce) package semi-sweet chocolate chips. Remove from heat; gently stir in 2½ cups oven-toasted rice cereal until completely coated. Press on bottom and up side to rim of buttered 9-inch or 10-inch pie plate. Chill 30 minutes.

LEMON ICEBOX CAKE

Makes 6 to 8 servings

1½ cups chocolate wafer cookie crumbs (about 30 wafers)
3 tablespoons margarine or butter, melted
¼ cup plus 3 tablespoons sugar
1 (14-ounce) can Eagle® Brand Sweetened Condensed Milk (NOT evaporated milk)
2 eggs,* separated
½ cup ReaLemon® Lemon Juice from Concentrate
1 tablespoon grated lemon rind, optional
1 cup (½ pint) whipping cream, whipped

Line 9×5-inch loaf pan with aluminum foil, extending foil above sides of pan; butter foil. Combine crumbs, margarine and 3 tablespoons sugar. Press firmly on bottom and up sides of prepared pan. In large mixer bowl, beat sweetened condensed milk and egg yolks until well blended. Add ReaLemon and rind if desired. In small mixer bowl, beat egg whites until soft peaks form; gradually add remaining ¼ cup sugar, beating until stiff but not dry. Fold into sweetened condensed milk mixture along with whipped cream. Pour into prepared pan; cover. Freeze at least 8 hours or until firm. To serve, remove from pan; peel off foil and slice. Return leftovers to freezer.

*Use only Grade A clean, uncracked eggs.

FROZEN STRAWBERRY MARGARITA PIE

Makes one 9-inch pie

1¼ cups *finely* crushed pretzel crumbs
  ½ cup plus 2 tablespoons margarine or
    butter, melted
  ¼ cup sugar
  1 (14-ounce) can Eagle® Brand
    Sweetened Condensed Milk
    (NOT evaporated milk)
  1 cup chopped fresh or frozen
    unsweetened strawberries, thawed
  ¼ cup ReaLime® Lime Juice from
    Concentrate
  3 to 4 tablespoons tequila
  2 tablespoons triple sec or other
    orange-flavored liqueur
  2 to 4 drops red food coloring, optional
  1 cup (½ pint) whipping cream,
    whipped

Combine crumbs, margarine and sugar; press firmly on bottom and up side of lightly buttered 9-inch pie plate. In large mixing bowl, combine sweetened condensed milk, chopped strawberries, ReaLime, tequila, triple sec and food coloring if desired; mix well. Fold in whipped cream. Pour into prepared crust. Freeze 4 hours or until firm. Let stand 10 minutes before serving. Garnish as desired. Return leftovers to freezer.

Margarita Pie: Omit strawberries and red food coloring. Increase ReaLime to ⅓ cup. Proceed as above. Freeze 4 hours or chill 2 hours. Garnish as desired. Return leftovers to freezer or refrigerator.

◄TORTONI

Makes 1½ to 2 dozen

1 (14-ounce) can Eagle® Brand
   Sweetened Condensed Milk
   (NOT evaporated milk)
3 egg yolks,* beaten
¼ cup light rum
2 teaspoons vanilla extract
⅔ cup coconut macaroon crumbs (about
   5 macaroons)
½ to ¾ cup slivered almonds, toasted
⅓ to ½ cup chopped maraschino
   cherries
2 cups (1 pint) whipping cream,
   whipped

In large mixing bowl, combine all ingredients
except whipped cream; mix well. Fold in
whipped cream. Fill 2½-inch foil cups; cover.
Freeze 6 hours or until firm. Garnish as
desired. Return leftovers to freezer.

*Use only Grade A clean, uncracked eggs.

FROZEN ORANGE CREAM

Makes about 1 quart

2 cups (1 pint) coffee cream
1 (14-ounce) can Eagle® Brand
   Sweetened Condensed Milk
   (NOT evaporated milk)
1 (6-ounce) can frozen orange juice
   concentrate, thawed
1 cup cold water
1 teaspoon grated orange rind

In large mixing bowl, combine ingredients; mix
well. Pour into 8-inch square pan; cover. Freeze
4 hours or until firm. Remove from freezer 5
minutes before serving. Return leftovers to
freezer.

Frozen Lemon Cream: Omit orange juice
concentrate and orange rind. Use ½ cup
ReaLemon® Lemon Juice from Concentrate
and 1 teaspoon grated lemon rind. Proceed as
above.

MUD PIE ▲

Makes one 9-inch pie

- 1 (14-ounce) can Eagle® Brand Sweetened Condensed Milk (NOT evaporated milk)
- 3 egg yolks*
- 4 teaspoons vanilla extract
- 1 cup coarsely crushed creme-filled chocolate sandwich cookies (12 cookies)
- 2 cups (1 pint) whipping cream, whipped (do not use non-dairy whipped topping)
- 1 (9-inch) chocolate crumb crust
  Chocolate fudge ice cream topping or chocolate flavored syrup
  Chopped nuts

In large mixer bowl, beat sweetened condensed milk, egg yolks and vanilla until well blended. Fold in cookies and whipped cream. Pour into 9×5-inch loaf pan or other 2-quart container; cover. Freeze 6 hours or until firm. Scoop ice cream into prepared crust. Drizzle with topping. Garnish with nuts. Return leftovers to freezer.

*Use only Grade A clean, uncracked eggs.

LEMON DESSERT FREEZE

Makes 9 servings

- 3 tablespoons margarine or butter, melted
- 1 cup graham cracker crumbs
- 1 (21- or 22-ounce) can lemon pie filling
- 1 (14-ounce) can Eagle® Brand Sweetened Condensed Milk (NOT evaporated milk)
- ½ cup ReaLemon® Lemon Juice from Concentrate
- 1½ cups frozen non-dairy whipped topping, thawed

Combine margarine and crumbs. Reserving 1 tablespoon crumbs for garnish, press remainder firmly on bottom of 8- or 9-inch square pan; set aside. In medium mixing bowl, combine pie filling, sweetened condensed milk and ReaLemon; stir until smooth. Spread into prepared pan. Spread whipped topping over top; garnish with reserved crumbs. Freeze 4 hours or until firm. Garnish as desired. Cut into squares to serve. Return leftovers to freezer.

Pour ice cream mixture into aluminum foil-lined round bowl.

Invert ice cream layer on brownie layer; peel off foil.

Spread meringue completely over ice cream and brownie, sealing carefully to edge of brownie.

◄ GRASSHOPPER BAKED ALASKA

Makes 12 to 15 servings

ICE CREAM:
  1 (14-ounce) can Eagle® Brand
    Sweetened Condensed Milk
    (NOT evaporated milk)
  ⅓ cup green creme de menthe
  ¼ cup white creme de cacao
  2 cups (1 pint) whipping cream,
    whipped (do not use non-dairy
    whipped topping)
  ½ cup mini chocolate chips

BROWNIE:
  1 (15- or 15½-ounce) package brownie
    mix

MERINGUE:
  4 egg whites*
  ¼ teaspoon cream of tartar
  ½ cup sugar
  1 tablespoon unsweetened cocoa

1. To prepare ice cream, in large mixing bowl, combine sweetened condensed milk and liqueurs. Fold in whipped cream and chips. Pour into aluminum foil-lined 2- or 3-quart round mixing bowl. Cover; freeze 8 to 12 hours or until firm.

2. Prepare brownie mix according to package directions. Pour into greased 8-inch round layer cake pan; bake according to package directions. Remove from pan; cool thoroughly.

3. Preheat oven to 500°. In large mixer bowl, beat egg whites and cream of tartar until soft peaks form. Gradually beat in sugar combined with cocoa until stiff but not dry. Place prepared brownie layer on ovenproof plate, wooden board or baking sheet. Remove ice cream from bowl; invert onto brownie layer. Trim to fit if desired. Quickly spread meringue over ice cream and brownie, sealing carefully to bottom edge of brownie. Bake 2 to 3 minutes or until lightly browned. Return to freezer; freeze at least 6 hours before serving. Return leftovers to freezer.

Tip: Alaska should be made several days ahead.

*Use only Grade A clean, uncracked eggs.

FUDGY CHOCOLATE ICE CREAM

Makes about 1½ quarts

  2 (1-ounce) squares unsweetened or
    semi-sweet chocolate
  1 (14-ounce) can Eagle® Brand
    Sweetened Condensed Milk
    (NOT evaporated milk)
  3 cups (1½ pints) coffee cream
  1 tablespoon vanilla extract

In medium saucepan, over low heat, melt chocolate with sweetened condensed milk; continue cooking until mixture thickens. Remove from heat; cool. Add remaining ingredients; mix well. Place in ice cream freezer container. Freeze according to manufacturer's instructions. Return leftovers to freezer.

Refrigerator-Freezer Method: Place combined ingredients in 13×9-inch baking pan; cover and freeze to a firm mush, about 1 hour. Break into pieces and turn into chilled large mixer bowl; beat until smooth. Return to pan. Cover; freeze until firm.

Tip: Recipe can be doubled.

SPIRITED MOCHA MOUSSE

Makes 10 to 12 servings

  1 tablespoon instant coffee
  1 teaspoon hot water
  1 (6-ounce) package semi-sweet
    chocolate chips
  1 (14-ounce) can Eagle® Brand
    Sweetened Condensed Milk
    (NOT evaporated milk)
  ¼ cup coffee-flavored liqueur, optional
  2 cups (1 pint) whipping cream,
    whipped (do not use non-dairy
    whipped topping)

In small bowl, dissolve coffee in water; set aside. In medium saucepan, melt chips; remove from heat. Stir in sweetened condensed milk, coffee liquid and liqueur if desired; mix well. Fold in whipped cream. Spoon about ½ cup mixture into 6-ounce dessert dishes; cover. Freeze 2 hours or until firm. Garnish as desired. Return leftovers to freezer.

FROZEN FLUFFY ▲ STRAWBERRY PIE

Makes one 9-inch pie

2½ cups flaked coconut, toasted
⅓ cup margarine or butter, melted
1 (3-ounce) package cream cheese, softened
1 (14-ounce) can Eagle® Brand Sweetened Condensed Milk (NOT evaporated milk)
2½ cups fresh or frozen unsweetened strawberries (thawed), mashed or pureed (about 1½ cups)
3 tablespoons ReaLemon® Lemon Juice from Concentrate
1 cup (½ pint) whipping cream, whipped
   Additional fresh strawberries, optional

Combine coconut and margarine; press firmly on bottom and up side to rim of 9-inch pie plate. In large mixer bowl, beat cheese until fluffy; gradually beat in sweetened condensed milk. Stir in pureed strawberries and ReaLemon. Fold in whipped cream. Pour into prepared crust (mixture should mound slightly). Freeze 4 hours or until firm. Before serving, garnish with fresh strawberries if desired. Return leftovers to freezer.

Tip: 1 (9-inch) baked pastry shell can be substituted for coconut crust.

FROZEN AMARETTO TORTE

Makes 12 to 15 servings

⅓ cup margarine or butter, melted
2 cups chocolate wafer cookie crumbs (about 40 wafers)
½ cup slivered almonds, toasted and chopped
1 (6-ounce) package butterscotch flavored chips
1 (14-ounce) can Eagle® Brand Sweetened Condensed Milk (NOT evaporated milk)
1 (16-ounce) container sour cream
⅓ cup amaretto or other almond-flavored liqueur
1 cup (½ pint) whipping cream, whipped

Combine margarine, crumbs and almonds. Reserving 1½ cups crumbs, press remainder firmly on bottom of 9-inch springform pan. In small saucepan, over medium heat, melt chips with sweetened condensed milk. In large mixing bowl, combine sour cream and amaretto; mix well. Stir in butterscotch mixture. Fold in whipped cream. Pour half the amaretto mixture over prepared crust; top with 1 cup reserved crumbs then remaining amaretto mixture. Top with remaining ½ cup crumbs; cover. Freeze 6 hours or until firm. Return leftovers to freezer.

EASY CHOCOLATE ICE CREAM 'N' CAKE ▶

Makes 12 servings

1 (18¼- or 18½-ounce) package white cake mix
1 (14-ounce) can Eagle® Brand Sweetened Condensed Milk (NOT evaporated milk)
⅔ cup chocolate flavored syrup
1 cup slivered almonds, toasted and chopped, optional
2 cups (1 pint) whipping cream, whipped (do not use non-dairy whipped topping)
1 (8-ounce) container frozen non-dairy whipped topping, thawed
Additional chocolate flavored syrup

Prepare and bake cake mix as directed for 13×9-inch cake. Cool slightly. Turn out on sheet of aluminum foil. Cool thoroughly; set aside. In large mixing bowl, combine sweetened condensed milk, ⅔ cup syrup and 1 cup chopped almonds. Fold in whipped cream. Line 13×9-inch baking pan with aluminum foil, extending foil above sides of pan. Pour chocolate mixture into prepared pan; cover. Freeze 6 hours or until firm. Lift ice cream out of pan with foil; turn out evenly on top of cake layer. Trim ice cream to fit cake layer. Quickly frost top and sides with whipped topping. Drizzle with chocolate syrup. Return to freezer at least 2 hours before serving. Return leftovers to freezer.

Tip: Can be made 2 weeks ahead.

VANILLA ICE CREAM

Makes about 3 quarts

4 eggs,* well beaten
6 cups (1½ quarts) coffee cream
2 (14-ounce) cans Eagle® Brand Sweetened Condensed Milk (NOT evaporated milk)
2 tablespoons vanilla extract

In ice cream freezer container, combine ingredients; mix well. Freeze according to manufacturer's instructions. Return leftovers to freezer.

Peach Ice Cream: Reduce vanilla to 1 tablespoon and add 1 teaspoon almond extract, 4 drops yellow and 2 drops red food coloring if desired and 2 cups mashed fresh or frozen peaches, thawed or 1 (16-ounce) can peaches, drained and mashed. Proceed as above.

Strawberry Ice Cream: Omit eggs. Reduce vanilla to 1 tablespoon. Add 2 cups mashed fresh or frozen strawberries, thawed and few drops red food coloring if desired. Proceed as above.

Banana Ice Cream: Reduce vanilla to 1 tablespoon; add 2 cups mashed bananas (4 medium). Proceed as above.

*Use only Grade A clean, uncracked eggs.

CANDIES & CONFECTIONS

Eagle Brand "magic" means rich creamy Foolproof Fudge every time—no long cooking, no candy thermometer needed. Choose your favorite flavor or try them all! Create your own gift box with colorful Fruit Bon Bons, candy critters, slices of Peanut Butter Logs, even spirited rum balls. From elegant, but easy Chocolate Truffles to Golden Snacking Granola, there's a sweet treat for everyone.

CARAMEL PEANUT BALLS

Makes about 4½ dozen

3 cups *finely* chopped dry roasted peanuts
1 (14-ounce) can Eagle® Brand Sweetened Condensed Milk (NOT evaporated milk)
1 teaspoon vanilla extract
½ pound chocolate confectioners' coating*

In heavy saucepan, combine nuts, sweetened condensed milk and vanilla. Over medium heat, cook and stir 8 to 10 minutes or until mixture forms ball around spoon and pulls away from side of pan. Cool 10 minutes. Chill if desired. Shape into 1-inch balls. In small heavy saucepan, over low heat, melt confectioners' coating. With wooden pick, dip each ball into melted coating, covering half of ball. Place on wax paper-lined baking sheets until firm. Store covered at room temperature or in refrigerator.

*Chocolate confectioners' coating can be purchased in candy specialty stores.

CHIPPER PEANUT CANDY

Makes about 2 pounds

1 (6-ounce) package butterscotch flavored chips
1 (14-ounce) can Eagle® Brand Sweetened Condensed Milk (NOT evaporated milk)
1 cup peanut butter
2 cups crushed potato chips
1 cup coarsely chopped peanuts

In heavy saucepan, melt butterscotch chips with sweetened condensed milk and peanut butter. Over medium heat, cook and stir until well blended. Remove from heat. Add potato chips and nuts; mix well. Press into aluminum foil-lined 8- or 9-inch square pan. Chill. Turn candy onto cutting board; peel off foil and cut into squares. Store loosely covered at room temperature.

MICROWAVE: In 2-quart glass measure, combine sweetened condensed milk, butterscotch chips and peanut butter. Microwave on full power (high) 4 minutes, stirring after 2 minutes. Proceed as above.

Top to Bottom: Apricot Almond Chewies (see page 78), Chipper Peanut Candy, Caramel Peanut Balls, Crunchy Clusters—Butterscotch and Chocolate (see page 78), Chipper Peanut Candy

CRUNCHY CLUSTERS

Makes about 3 dozen

- 1 (12-ounce) package semi-sweet chocolate chips *or* 3 (6-ounce) packages butterscotch flavored chips
- 1 (14-ounce) can Eagle® Brand Sweetened Condensed Milk (NOT evaporated milk)
- 1 (3-ounce) can chow mein noodles *or* 2 cups pretzel sticks, broken into ½-inch pieces
- 1 cup dry roasted peanuts *or* whole roasted almonds

In heavy saucepan, over low heat, melt chips with sweetened condensed milk. Remove from heat. In large mixing bowl, combine noodles and nuts; stir in chocolate mixture. Drop by tablespoonfuls onto wax paper-lined baking sheets; chill 2 hours or until firm. Store loosely covered in cool dry place.

MICROWAVE: In 2-quart glass measure, combine chips and sweetened condensed milk. Microwave on full power (high) 3 minutes, stirring after 1½ minutes. Stir until smooth. Proceed as above.

Chocolate Cherry Logs

APRICOT ALMOND CHEWIES

Makes about 6½ dozen

- 4 cups finely chopped dried apricots (about 1 pound)
- 4 cups flaked coconut or coconut macaroon crumbs (about 21 macaroons)
- 2 cups slivered almonds, toasted and finely chopped
- 1 (14-ounce) can Eagle® Brand Sweetened Condensed Milk (NOT evaporated milk)
  Whole almonds, optional

In large mixing bowl, combine all ingredients except whole almonds. Chill 2 hours. Shape into 1-inch balls. Top each with whole almond if desired. Store tightly covered in refrigerator.

CHOCOLATE CHERRY LOGS

Makes two 12-inch logs

- 3 (6-ounce) packages semi-sweet chocolate chips
- 1 (14-ounce) can Eagle® Brand Sweetened Condensed Milk (NOT evaporated milk)
- 1 (6-ounce) container candied cherries, chopped (about 1 cup)
- 1 teaspoon almond extract
- 1½ cups slivered almonds, toasted and chopped

In heavy saucepan, over low heat, melt chips with sweetened condensed milk. Remove from heat. Stir in cherries and extract. Chill 30 minutes. Divide in half; place each portion on a 20-inch piece of wax paper. Shape each into 12-inch log. Roll in nuts. Wrap tightly; chill 2 hours or until firm. Remove paper; cut into ¼-inch slices to serve. Store covered in refrigerator.

MICROWAVE: In 2-quart glass measure, combine chips and sweetened condensed milk. Microwave on full power (high) 3 minutes, stirring after 1½ minutes. Stir in cherries and extract. Chill 1 hour. Proceed as above.

GOLDEN SNACKING GRANOLA ▲

Makes about 2½ quarts

2 cups oats
1½ cups slivered almonds or coarsely chopped walnuts
1 (3½-ounce) can flaked coconut (1⅓ cups)
½ cup sunflower meats
½ cup wheat germ
2 tablespoons sesame seeds
1 teaspoon ground cinnamon
1 teaspoon salt
1 (14-ounce) can Eagle® Brand Sweetened Condensed Milk (NOT evaporated milk)
¼ cup vegetable oil
1 cup banana chips, optional
1 cup raisins

Preheat oven to 300°. In large mixing bowl, combine all ingredients except banana chips and raisins; mix well. Spread evenly in aluminum foil-lined 15×10-inch jellyroll pan or baking sheet. Bake 55 to 60 minutes, stirring every 15 minutes. Remove from oven; stir in banana chips if desired and raisins. Cool thoroughly. Store tightly covered at room temperature.

ROCKY ROAD CANDY

Makes about 3½ dozen

1 (12-ounce) package semi-sweet chocolate chips
2 tablespoons margarine or butter
1 (14-ounce) can Eagle® Brand Sweetened Condensed Milk (NOT evaporated milk)
2 cups dry roasted peanuts
1 (10½-ounce) package Campfire® Miniature Marshmallows

In heavy saucepan, over low heat, melt chips and margarine with sweetened condensed milk; remove from heat. In large mixing bowl, combine nuts and marshmallows; stir in chocolate mixture. Spread in wax paper-lined 13×9-inch pan. Chill 2 hours or until firm. Remove from pan; peel off wax paper and cut into squares. Store loosely covered at room temperature.

MICROWAVE: In 1-quart glass measure, combine chips, margarine and sweetened condensed milk. Microwave on full power (high) 3 minutes, stirring after 1½ minutes. Stir to melt chips. Let stand 5 minutes. Proceed as above.

Left to Right: Ginger Orange Nut Balls, Easy Peanut Butter Chocolate Fudge, Chocolate Fruit Balls, Scotchy Pecan Critters

SCOTCHY PECAN CRITTERS

Makes about 5 dozen

1 (6-ounce) package butterscotch
flavored chips
1 (14-ounce) can Eagle® Brand
Sweetened Condensed Milk
(NOT evaporated milk)
2 teaspoons white vinegar
4 cups pecan halves (¾ pound)
1 (11½-ounce) package milk chocolate
chips
1 teaspoon vanilla extract

In heavy saucepan, over low heat, melt butterscotch chips with *⅓ cup* sweetened condensed milk. Remove from heat; stir in vinegar. Drop by half teaspoonfuls onto wax paper-lined baking sheets. Arrange 3 pecans on each butterscotch drop. In large heavy saucepan, over low heat, melt milk chocolate chips with remaining sweetened condensed milk and vanilla. Remove from heat; hold chocolate mixture over hot water. Drop chocolate by heaping teaspoonfuls over pecan clusters. Chill 2 hours or until firm. Store loosely covered.

MICROWAVE: In 1-quart glass measure, combine butterscotch chips and *⅓ cup* sweetened condensed milk. Microwave on full power (high) 1½ minutes. Stir to melt chips. Add vinegar. Proceed as above. In 1-quart glass measure, combine milk chocolate chips with remaining sweetened condensed milk. Microwave on full power (high) 2 minutes. Stir to melt chips. Add vanilla. Proceed as above.

GINGER ORANGE NUT BALLS

Makes about 8 dozen

1 (16-ounce) package ginger snap
cookies, finely crushed (about
4 cups crumbs)
1 (14-ounce) can Eagle® Brand
Sweetened Condensed Milk
(NOT evaporated milk)
1 (3½-ounce) can flaked coconut
(1⅓ cups)
1 cup finely chopped nuts
1 cup raisins
⅓ cup orange juice
1 tablespoon grated orange rind
Additional flaked coconut and grated
orange rind

In large mixing bowl, combine all ingredients except additional coconut and rind. Chill at least 1 hour. Shape into 1-inch balls. Roll in additional coconut mixed with rind. Store tightly covered in refrigerator.

Tip: Flavor of these candies improves after 24 hours. They can be made ahead and stored in refrigerator for several weeks.

CHOCOLATE FRUIT BALLS

Makes about 8 dozen

2½ cups vanilla wafer crumbs (about 65 wafers)
1 (14-ounce) can Eagle® Brand Sweetened Condensed Milk (NOT evaporated milk)
1 (8-ounce) package chopped dates
1 cup finely chopped nuts
½ cup chopped candied cherries
2 tablespoons unsweetened cocoa
Confectioners' sugar *or* unsweetened cocoa
Additional candied cherries, optional

In large mixing bowl, combine all ingredients except confectioners' sugar and additional cherries; mix well. Chill 1 hour. Shape into 1-inch balls. Roll in confectioners' sugar. Store tightly covered in refrigerator. Garnish with additional candied cherries if desired.

Tip: Flavor of these candies improves after 24 hours. They can be made ahead and stored in refrigerator for several weeks.

EASY PEANUT BUTTER CHOCOLATE FUDGE

Makes about 2 pounds

1 (12-ounce) package peanut butter flavored chips
¼ cup margarine or butter
1 (14-ounce) can Eagle® Brand Sweetened Condensed Milk (NOT evaporated milk)
½ cup chopped peanuts, optional
1 (6-ounce) package semi-sweet chocolate chips

In heavy saucepan, melt peanut butter chips and *2 tablespoons* margarine with *1 cup* sweetened condensed milk. Remove from heat; stir in nuts if desired. Spread into wax paper-lined 8-inch square pan. In small heavy saucepan, melt chocolate chips and remaining *2 tablespoons* margarine with remaining sweetened condensed milk. Spread chocolate mixture on top of peanut butter mixture. Chill 2 hours or until firm. Turn fudge onto cutting board; peel off paper and cut into squares. Store loosely covered at room temperature.

FRUIT BON BONS

Makes about 5 dozen

1 (14-ounce) can Eagle® Brand Sweetened Condensed Milk (NOT evaporated milk)
2 (7-ounce) packages flaked coconut (5⅓ cups)
1 (6-ounce) package fruit flavor gelatin, any flavor
1 cup ground blanched almonds
1 teaspoon almond extract
Food coloring, optional

In large mixing bowl, combine sweetened condensed milk, coconut, ⅓ *cup* gelatin, almonds, extract and enough food coloring to tint mixture desired shade. Chill 1 hour or until firm enough to handle. Using about ½ tablespoon mixture for each, shape into 1-inch balls. Sprinkle remaining gelatin onto wax paper; roll each ball in gelatin to coat. Place on wax paper-lined baking sheets; chill. Store covered at room temperature or in refrigerator.

MILK CHOCOLATE BOURBON BALLS

Makes about 5½ dozen

1 (12-ounce) package vanilla wafer cookies, finely crushed (about 3 cups crumbs)
5 tablespoons bourbon or brandy
1 (11½-ounce) package milk chocolate chips
1 (14-ounce) can Eagle® Brand Sweetened Condensed Milk (NOT evaporated milk)
Finely chopped nuts

In medium mixing bowl, combine crumbs and bourbon. In heavy saucepan, over low heat, melt chips. Remove from heat; add sweetened condensed milk. Gradually add crumb mixture; mix well. Let stand at room temperature 30 minutes or chill. Shape into 1-inch balls; roll in nuts. Store tightly covered.

Tip: Flavor of these candies improves after 24 hours. They can be made ahead and stored in freezer. Thaw before serving.

FOOLPROOF DARK CHOCOLATE FUDGE

Makes about 2 pounds

> 3 (6-ounce) packages semi-sweet
>   chocolate chips
> 1 (14-ounce) can Eagle® Brand
>   Sweetened Condensed Milk
>   (NOT evaporated milk)
>   Dash salt
> ½ to 1 cup chopped nuts
> 1½ teaspoons vanilla extract

In heavy saucepan, over low heat, melt chips with sweetened condensed milk and salt. Remove from heat; stir in nuts and vanilla. Spread evenly into wax paper-lined 8- or 9-inch square pan. Chill 2 hours or until firm. Turn fudge onto cutting board; peel off paper and cut into squares. Store loosely covered at room temperature.

MICROWAVE: In 1-quart glass measure, combine chips with sweetened condensed milk. Microwave on full power (high) 3 minutes. Stir until chips melt and mixture is smooth. Stir in remaining ingredients. Proceed as above.

Creamy Dark Chocolate Fudge: Melt 2 cups Campfire® Miniature Marshmallows with chips and sweetened condensed milk. Proceed as above.

Milk Chocolate Fudge: Omit 1 (6-ounce) package semi-sweet chocolate chips. Add 1 cup milk chocolate chips. Proceed as above.

Creamy Milk Chocolate Fudge: Omit 1 (6-ounce) package semi-sweet chocolate chips. Add 1 cup milk chocolate chips and 2 cups Campfire® Miniature Marshmallows. Proceed as above.

Mexican Chocolate Fudge: Reduce vanilla to 1 teaspoon. Add 1 tablespoon instant coffee and 1 teaspoon ground cinnamon to sweetened condensed milk. Proceed as above.

Butterscotch Fudge: Omit chocolate chips and vanilla. In heavy saucepan, melt 2 (12-ounce) packages butterscotch flavored chips with sweetened condensed milk. Remove from heat; stir in 2 tablespoons white vinegar, ⅛ teaspoon salt, ½ teaspoon maple flavoring and 1 cup chopped nuts. Proceed as above.

BUCKEYES

Makes about 7 dozen

> 2 (3-ounce) packages cream cheese,
>   softened
> 1 (14-ounce) can Eagle® Brand
>   Sweetened Condensed Milk
>   (NOT evaporated milk)
> 2 (12-ounce) packages peanut butter
>   flavored chips
> 1 cup finely chopped peanuts
> ½ pound chocolate confectioners'
>   coating*

In large mixer bowl, beat cheese until fluffy. Gradually beat in sweetened condensed milk until smooth. In heavy saucepan, over low heat, melt peanut butter chips; stir into cheese mixture. Add nuts. Chill 2 to 3 hours; shape into 1-inch balls. In small heavy saucepan, over low heat, melt confectioners' coating. With wooden pick, dip each peanut ball into melted coating, not covering completely. Place on wax paper-lined baking sheets until firm. Store covered at room temperature or in refrigerator.

*Chocolate confectioners' coating can be purchased in candy specialty stores.

COCONUT RUM BALLS

Makes about 8 dozen

> 1 (12-ounce) package vanilla wafer
>   cookies, finely crushed (about
>   3 cups crumbs)
> 1 (3½-ounce) can flaked coconut
>   (1⅓ cups)
> 1 cup finely chopped nuts
> 1 (14-ounce) can Eagle® Brand
>   Sweetened Condensed Milk
>   (NOT evaporated milk)
> ¼ cup rum
>   Additional flaked coconut or
>   confectioners' sugar

In large mixing bowl, combine crumbs, coconut and nuts. Add sweetened condensed milk and rum; mix well. Chill 4 hours. Shape into 1-inch balls. Roll in coconut. Store tightly covered in refrigerator.

Tip: Flavor of these candies improves after 24 hours. They can be made ahead and stored in refrigerator for several weeks.

LAYERED MINT CHOCOLATE CANDY

Makes about 1¾ pounds

- 1 (12-ounce) package semi-sweet chocolate chips
- 1 (14-ounce) can Eagle® Brand Sweetened Condensed Milk (NOT evaporated milk)
- 2 teaspoons vanilla extract
- 6 ounces white confectioners' coating*
- 1 tablespoon peppermint extract
  Few drops green or red food coloring, optional

In heavy saucepan, over low heat, melt chips with *1 cup* sweetened condensed milk. Stir in vanilla. Spread half the mixture into wax paper-lined 8- or 9-inch square pan; chill 10 minutes or until firm. Hold remaining chocolate mixture at room temperature. In heavy saucepan, over low heat, melt coating with remaining sweetened condensed milk. Stir in peppermint extract and food coloring if desired. Spread on chilled chocolate layer; chill 10 minutes longer or until firm. Spread reserved chocolate mixture on mint layer. Chill 2 hours or until firm. Turn onto cutting board; peel off paper and cut into squares. Store loosely covered at room temperature.

*White confectioners' coating can be purchased in candy specialty stores.

Clockwise from Top: Coconut Rum Balls (see page 82), Chocolate Pecan Critters (see page 84), Fruit Bon Bons (see page 81), Milk Chocolate Bourbon Balls (see page 81), Buckeyes (see page 82), Foolproof Dark Chocolate Fudge (see page 82), Peanut Butter Logs (see page 84), Layered Mint Chocolate Candy (see page 83), Creamy White Cherry Fudge (see page 84)

CREAMY WHITE FUDGE

Makes about 2¼ pounds

1½ pounds white confectioners' coating*
**1 (14-ounce) can Eagle® Brand
    Sweetened Condensed Milk
    (NOT evaporated milk)**
⅛ teaspoon salt
¾ to 1 cup chopped nuts
1½ teaspoons vanilla extract

In heavy saucepan, over low heat, melt coating with sweetened condensed milk and salt. Remove from heat; stir in nuts and vanilla. Spread evenly into wax paper-lined 8- or 9-inch square pan. Chill 2 hours or until firm. Turn fudge onto cutting board; peel off paper and cut into squares. Store tightly covered at room temperature.

MICROWAVE: In 2-quart glass measure, combine coating, sweetened condensed milk and salt. Microwave on full power (high) 3 to 5 minutes or until coating melts, stirring after 3 minutes. Stir in nuts and vanilla. Proceed as above.

Praline Fudge: Omit vanilla. Add 1 teaspoon maple flavoring and 1 cup chopped pecans. Proceed as above.

Confetti Fudge: Omit nuts. Add 1 cup chopped mixed candied fruit. Proceed as above.

Rum Raisin Fudge: Omit vanilla. Add 1½ teaspoons white vinegar, 1 teaspoon rum flavoring and ¾ cup raisins. Proceed as above.

Cherry Fudge: Omit nuts. Add 1 cup chopped candied cherries.

*White confectioners' coating can be purchased in candy specialty stores.

PEANUT BUTTER LOGS

Makes two 12-inch logs

**1 (12-ounce) package peanut butter
    flavored chips**
**1 (14-ounce) can Eagle® Brand
    Sweetened Condensed Milk
    (NOT evaporated milk)**
**1 cup Campfire® Miniature
    Marshmallows**
1 cup chopped peanuts

In heavy saucepan, over low heat, melt chips with sweetened condensed milk. Add marshmallows; stir until melted. Remove from heat; cool 20 minutes. Divide in half; place each portion on a 20-inch piece of wax paper. Shape each into 12-inch log. Roll in nuts. Wrap tightly; chill 2 hours or until firm. Remove paper; cut into ¼-inch slices.

MICROWAVE: In 2-quart glass measure, microwave chips, sweetened condensed milk and marshmallows on full power (high) 4 minutes or until melted, stirring after 2 minutes. Let stand at room temperature 1 hour. Proceed as above.

Peanut Butter Fudge: Stir peanuts into mixture. Spread into wax paper-lined 8- or 9-inch square pan. Chill 2 hours or until firm. Turn fudge onto cutting board; peel off paper and cut into squares.

CHOCOLATE PECAN CRITTERS

Makes about 5 dozen

**1 (11½-ounce) package milk chocolate
    chips**
**1 (6-ounce) package semi-sweet
    chocolate chips**
¼ cup margarine or butter
**1 (14-ounce) can Eagle® Brand
    Sweetened Condensed Milk
    (NOT evaporated milk)**
⅛ teaspoon salt
2 cups coarsely chopped pecans
**2 teaspoons vanilla extract
    Pecan halves**

In heavy saucepan, over medium heat, melt chips and margarine with sweetened condensed milk and salt. Remove from heat; stir in chopped nuts and vanilla. Drop by teaspoonfuls onto wax paper-lined baking sheets. Top with pecan halves. Chill. Store tightly covered.

MICROWAVE: In 2-quart glass measure, microwave chips, margarine, sweetened condensed milk and salt on full power (high) 3 minutes, stirring after 1½ minutes. Stir to melt chips; stir in chopped nuts and vanilla. Proceed as above.

CHOCOLATE TRUFFLES ▶

Makes about 6 dozen

3 (6-ounce) packages semi-sweet
   chocolate chips
1 (14-ounce) can Eagle® Brand
   Sweetened Condensed Milk
   (NOT evaporated milk)
1 tablespoon vanilla extract
   Finely chopped nuts, flaked coconut,
   chocolate sprinkles, colored
   sprinkles, unsweetened cocoa *or*
   colored sugar

In heavy saucepan, over low heat, melt chips
with sweetened condensed milk. Remove from
heat; stir in vanilla. Chill 2 hours or until firm.
Shape into 1-inch balls; roll in any of the above
coatings. Chill 1 hour or until firm. Store
covered at room temperature.

MICROWAVE: In 1-quart glass measure,
combine chips and sweetened condensed milk.
Microwave on full power (high) 3 minutes,
stirring after 1½ minutes. Stir until smooth.
Proceed as above.

Amaretto: Omit vanilla. Add 3 tablespoons
amaretto or other almond-flavored liqueur and
½ teaspoon almond extract. Roll in finely
chopped toasted almonds.

Orange: Omit vanilla. Add 3 tablespoons
orange-flavored liqueur. Roll in finely chopped
toasted almonds mixed with finely grated
orange rind.

Rum: Omit vanilla. Add ¼ cup dark rum. Roll
in flaked coconut.

Bourbon: Omit vanilla. Add 3 tablespoons
bourbon. Roll in finely chopped toasted nuts.

TOASTED VIENNA CHUNKS

Makes about 5 dozen

½ loaf Vienna or French bread, cut into
   1-inch cubes
1 (14-ounce) can Eagle® Brand
   Sweetened Condensed Milk
   (NOT evaporated milk)
1 (7-ounce) package flaked coconut
   (2⅔ cups)

Preheat oven to 350°. Dip bread into sweetened
condensed milk; allow to drain briefly. Roll in
coconut. Place on aluminum foil-lined and
greased baking sheets; bake 8 minutes or until
coconut is toasted. *Immediately* remove from
baking sheets. Store loosely covered at room
temperature.

Tip: For a campfire treat, toast chunks over
open fire.

BEVERAGES

The creamy goodness of Eagle Brand makes it the perfect base for punches and beverages. For kids of all ages, whip up a fruit shake that stays thick and smooth in the refrigerator. Make any occasion special with Coffee Egg Nog or Grasshopper Punch. Instead of dessert, sip your favorite flavor of Homemade Cream Liqueur!

BRANDY MILK PUNCH

Makes about 3 quarts

5 cups cold milk
2 (14-ounce) cans Eagle® Brand Sweetened Condensed Milk (NOT evaporated milk)
1 to 1½ cups brandy
1 cup light rum
3 egg whites*
Nutmeg

In large punch bowl, combine milk and sweetened condensed milk; add brandy and rum. In small bowl, beat egg whites to soft peaks. Stir into milk mixture. Chill. Garnish with nutmeg. Refrigerate leftovers.

*Use only Grade A clean, uncracked eggs.

CREAMY HOT CHOCOLATE   ▶

Makes about 2 quarts

1 (14-ounce) can Eagle® Brand Sweetened Condensed Milk (NOT evaporated milk)
½ cup unsweetened cocoa
1½ teaspoons vanilla extract
⅛ teaspoon salt
6½ cups hot water
Marshmallows, optional

In large saucepan, combine sweetened condensed milk, cocoa, vanilla and salt; mix well. Over medium heat, slowly stir in water; heat through, stirring occasionally. DO NOT BOIL. Top with marshmallows if desired.

MICROWAVE: In 2-quart glass measure, combine all ingredients except marshmallows. Microwave on full power (high) 8 to 10 minutes, stirring every 3 minutes. Top with marshmallows if desired.

Tip: Chocolate can be stored in refrigerator up to 5 days. Mix well and reheat before serving.

BANANA SHAKE ▶

Makes about 5 cups

2 ripe bananas, cut up (about 2 cups)
1 (14-ounce) can Eagle® Brand
   Sweetened Condensed Milk
   (NOT evaporated milk)
1 cup cold water
⅓ cup ReaLemon® Lemon Juice from
   Concentrate
2 cups ice cubes

In blender container, combine all ingredients except ice; blend well. Gradually add ice, blending until smooth. Garnish as desired. Refrigerate leftovers. (Mixture stays thick and creamy in refrigerator.)

Strawberry: Omit bananas. Add 1 pint fresh strawberries, cleaned and hulled *or* 2 cups frozen unsweetened strawberries, partially thawed and few drops red food coloring if desired. Proceed as above.

Orange-Banana: Omit 1 banana and reduce ReaLemon to ¼ cup. Add 1 (6-ounce) can frozen orange juice concentrate, thawed. Proceed as above.

Pineapple: Omit bananas. Add 1 (8-ounce) can crushed juice-packed pineapple. Proceed as above.

Mixer Method: Omit ice cubes. In large mixer bowl, mash fruit; gradually beat in ReaLemon, sweetened condensed milk and 2½ cups cold water. Chill before serving.

GRASSHOPPER PUNCH

Makes about 2½ quarts

1 (14-ounce) can Eagle® Brand
   Sweetened Condensed Milk
   (NOT evaporated milk)
½ cup green creme de menthe
½ cup white creme de cacao
2 (32-ounce) bottles club soda, chilled
   Mint chocolate chip ice cream

In punch bowl, combine sweetened condensed milk, creme de menthe and creme de cacao; mix well. Slowly pour in club soda. Top with scoops of ice cream.

CREAMY PINK PUNCH

Makes about 3½ quarts

2 (14-ounce) cans Eagle® Brand
   Sweetened Condensed Milk
   (NOT evaporated milk)
1 to 1½ cups kirsch or other cherry-
   flavored liqueur
¼ cup grenadine syrup
2 (32-ounce) bottles club soda, chilled
   Cherry vanilla ice cream

In large punch bowl, combine sweetened condensed milk, kirsch and grenadine. Just before serving, gradually add club soda; stir. Top with scoops of ice cream.

Homemade Cream Liqueurs—Coffee (left), Orange (middle), Mint (right)

HOMEMADE CREAM LIQUEURS

Makes about 1 quart

1 (14-ounce) can Eagle® Brand
    Sweetened Condensed Milk
    (NOT evaporated milk)
1¼ cups flavored liqueur (almond, coffee,
    orange *or* mint)
1 cup (½ pint) whipping or coffee
    cream
4 eggs*

In blender container, combine all ingredients;
blend until smooth. Serve over ice and garnish
if desired. Store tightly covered in refrigerator
up to 1 month. Stir before serving.

Mixer Method: In large mixer bowl, beat
eggs; beat in remaining ingredients until
smooth and well blended. Proceed as above.

*Use only Grade A clean, uncracked eggs.

COFFEE EGG NOG PUNCH

Makes about 1½ quarts

3 cups cold milk
1 (14-ounce) can Eagle® Brand
    Sweetened Condensed Milk
    (NOT evaporated milk)
4 eggs*
3 to 4 teaspoons instant coffee
⅓ cup bourbon
⅓ cup coffee-flavored liqueur
1 cup (½ pint) whipping cream,
    whipped
    Dash ground cinnamon
    Dash ground nutmeg

In large mixer bowl, combine milk, sweetened
condensed milk, eggs and coffee; beat on low
speed until coffee dissolves. Stir in bourbon
and liqueur; chill. Before serving, top with
whipped cream, cinnamon and nutmeg.
Refrigerate leftovers.

Holiday Egg Nog: Omit instant coffee and
coffee-flavored liqueur. Increase bourbon to ½
cup; add 1 teaspoon vanilla extract. Proceed as
above.

*Use only Grade A clean, uncracked eggs.

ORANGE PINEAPPLE PUNCH

Makes about 4 quarts

- 1 (46-ounce) can pineapple juice, chilled
- 1½ cups light rum, optional
- 1 (14-ounce) can Eagle® Brand Sweetened Condensed Milk (NOT evaporated milk)
- 1 (6-ounce) can frozen orange juice concentrate, thawed
- 2 (32-ounce) bottles ginger ale, chilled Orange sherbet, orange slices and mint leaves

In large punch bowl, combine all ingredients except ginger ale and sherbet. Just before serving, gradually add ginger ale; stir. Top with scoops of sherbet, orange slices and mint.

HOMEMADE IRISH CREAM LIQUEUR

Makes about 5 cups

- 1¼ to 1¾ cups liquor (Irish whiskey, brandy, rum, bourbon, scotch *or* rye whiskey)
- 1 (14-ounce) can Eagle® Brand Sweetened Condensed Milk (NOT evaporated milk)
- 1 cup (½ pint) whipping or coffee cream
- 4 eggs*
- 2 tablespoons chocolate flavored syrup
- 2 teaspoons instant coffee
- 1 teaspoon vanilla extract
- ½ teaspoon almond extract

In blender container, combine all ingredients; blend until smooth. Serve over ice if desired. Store tightly covered in refrigerator up to 1 month. Stir before serving.

Mixer Method: In large mixer bowl, beat eggs; beat in remaining ingredients until smooth and well blended. Proceed as above.

*Use only Grade A clean, uncracked eggs.

Orange Pineapple Punch

DESSERT MAKING HINTS

INTRODUCTION

Eagle® Brand Sweetened Condensed Milk is an all-natural concentrated blend of whole milk and cane sugar condensed by a special vacuum cooking process. It is entirely different from evaporated milk. Eagle Brand may become thicker and more caramel-colored as its age or storage temperature increases. The performance of the product is not affected by these natural changes. The unopened product is safe and wholesome indefinitely as long as the can seal is intact. If the sweetened condensed milk becomes unusually thick, stir briskly before using. If the product has become very caramelized, use in recipes where the caramel flavor is compatible with other ingredients. The best storage for sweetened condensed milk is a cool, dry place.

Because it is a natural product, Eagle Brand may vary in color and consistency from can to can. These two photos below illustrate the normal differences which may occur in Eagle Brand over time.

HINTS FOR USING EAGLE BRAND

- Remove entire end of can with can opener; then use rubber scraper to remove all of the sweetened condensed milk from the can.
- To avoid lumps in a cream cheese base recipe, gradually beat sweetened condensed milk into beaten cream cheese.
- Always heat sweetened condensed milk and chocolate over low or medium heat, stirring constantly.
- To avoid lumpy gelatine mixtures, sprinkle unflavored gelatine over cold water; let stand 1 minute. Cook and stir over *low* heat until dissolved.
- Always store any unused sweetened condensed milk in refrigerator in covered container. Use within a week.

EAGLE BRAND IS PRESWEETENED

Because Eagle Brand contains sugar which has already been thoroughly dissolved in the manufacturing process, most Eagle Brand recipes require no additional sugar.

EAGLE BRAND & CHOCOLATE

When heated with chocolate, Eagle Brand quickly thickens to a velvety smooth consistency for candies and sauces that are never grainy or long-cooking. There's no need for constant stirring or a candy thermometer.

ICE CREAM MAKING

The thick creamy consistency of Eagle Brand helps to minimize the formation of large ice crystals in ice creams and frozen desserts.

MAGIC THICKENING

Because it is a precooked blend of milk and sugar, Eagle Brand thickens almost magically with the addition of acidic fruit juices—to form delicious pie fillings, puddings and desserts *without cooking*. Lemon juice or orange juice concentrate works best.

A NOTE ABOUT EGGS

Some recipes in this book specify, "Use only Grade A clean, uncracked eggs." This is a precaution given when uncooked eggs are called for—egg nog, meringues, pie fillings.

TINTING COCONUT

Dilute few drops food coloring with ½ teaspoon water or milk. Add coconut; toss with fork until evenly tinted.

TOASTING COCONUT AND NUTS

Spread coconut or nuts evenly in shallow pan. Toast in preheated 350° oven 7 to 15 minutes or until golden, stirring frequently.

CHOCOLATE LEAVES

Coat undersides of real leaves lightly with vegetable oil. Melt semi-sweet chocolate and coat undersides of leaves thickly with chocolate using small spoon. Chill or freeze until firm, then peel away leaf.

CHOCOLATE CURLS

With a vegetable parer or thin, sharp knife, slice across block of sweet milk chocolate or large-size milk chocolate candy bar with long, thin strokes. Chocolate should be at room temperature.

PASTRY EGG WASH

For a more golden crust on a 2-crust pie, beat 1 egg yolk with 2 tablespoons water; brush evenly over pastry before baking.

FROSTING GRAPES

Dip small clusters of grapes into slightly beaten egg white; sprinkle with granulated sugar. Dry on wire racks.

HOW TO CARAMELIZE EAGLE BRAND*

Oven Method: Preheat oven to 425°. Pour 1 (14-ounce) can Eagle® Brand Sweetened Condensed Milk into 8- or 9-inch pie plate. Cover with aluminum foil; place in shallow pan. Fill pan with hot water. Bake 1 to 1½ hours or until thick and light caramel-colored. Remove foil; cool. Chill thoroughly. Refrigerate leftovers.

Stovetop Method: Pour 1 (14-ounce) can Eagle® Brand Sweetened Condensed Milk into top of double boiler; cover. Place over boiling water. Simmer 1 to 1½ hours or until thick and light caramel-colored. Beat until smooth. Cool. Chill thoroughly. Refrigerate leftovers.

Microwave Method: Pour 1 (14-ounce) can Eagle® Brand Sweetened Condensed Milk into 2-quart glass measure. Microwave on ½ power (medium) 4 minutes, stirring briskly after 2 minutes. Reduce to ⅓ power (low); microwave 12 to 16 minutes or until thick and light caramel-colored, stirring briskly every 2 minutes until smooth. Chill thoroughly. Refrigerate leftovers.

Serve caramelized Eagle Brand with fruit, chopped nuts, whipped cream or shaved chocolate.

*CAUTION: NEVER HEAT UNOPENED CAN.

To marble, gently swirl a narrow spatula through the light and dark mixtures.

PASTRY CRUST

Makes one 8- or 9-inch crust

1 cup unsifted flour
½ teaspoon salt
⅓ cup shortening
3 to 4 tablespoons cold water

In medium mixing bowl, combine flour and salt; cut in shortening until mixture resembles coarse cornmeal. Sprinkle with water, 1 tablespoon at a time, mixing until dough is just moist enough to hold together. Form dough into ball. Place on well-floured surface. Press down into a flat circle with smooth edges. Roll dough to a circle ⅛-inch thick and about 1½ inches larger than inverted pie plate. Ease dough into pie plate. Trim ½ inch beyond pie plate edge. Fold under; flute edge as desired.

TO BAKE WITHOUT FILLING

Preheat oven to 450°. Prick bottom and side of pastry shell with fork. Line pastry with aluminum foil; fill with dry beans. Bake 5 minutes; remove beans and foil. Bake 5 to 7 minutes longer or until golden.

TO BAKE WITH FILLING

Preheat oven as directed in recipe. Do not prick pastry shell. Fill and bake as directed.

CRUMB CRUST

Makes one 8- or 9-inch crust

1½ cups graham cracker or chocolate wafer crumbs
¼ cup sugar
6 tablespoons margarine or butter, melted

Combine ingredients; mix well. Press firmly on bottom and up side to rim of 8- or 9-inch pie plate. Chill thoroughly or bake in preheated 375° oven 6 to 8 minutes or until edges are brown. Cool before filling.

FOR BAKED ALASKAS

Ice cream must be very firm before it is covered with meringue and baked. Dessert can be frozen several days before serving.

WHIPPING CREAM

- Chill beaters and bowl thoroughly.
- Beat chilled whipping cream on high speed (overbeating or beating on low speed can cause cream to separate into fat and liquid).
- Beat only until stiff. Whipping cream doubles in volume.
- To sweeten whipped cream, gradually beat in 1 to 2 tablespoons granulated or confectioners' sugar and ½ to 1 teaspoon vanilla extract for each cup unwhipped whipping cream.

MAKE-AHEAD WHIPPED CREAM

Freeze dollops of whipped cream on wax paper-lined baking sheets. When frozen, store in tightly closed plastic bags for use on desserts or Irish coffee.

SLICING HINTS

- Use a wet knife for cutting desserts with meringue. Wipe off knife after each cut.
- Use a damp knife with a thin blade for slicing cake rolls.
- Use a damp knife with a firm blade for cutting fudge or candy.
- Use a serrated knife for slicing angel food cakes.

FOR SUCCESSFUL MERINGUE

- Weather affects meringues. When the humidity is high, sugar in the meringue absorbs moisture from the air, making the meringue gooey and limp. Meringues should be made on sunny, dry days.
- Carefully separate the egg whites from the yolks (they separate best when cold).
- Mixing bowls and beaters should be completely grease-free.
- Egg whites should come to room temperature before beating. This increases the volume.
- Sugar should be added *gradually*. Continue beating until sugar is completely dissolved.
- Cool meringue slowly, away from drafts to prevent shrinking and weeping.

MERINGUE

For 8- or 9-inch pie

3 egg whites*
¼ teaspoon cream of tartar
6 tablespoons sugar

Preheat oven to 350°. In small mixer bowl, beat egg whites with cream of tartar until soft peaks form; gradually add sugar, beating until stiff but not dry. Spread meringue on top of pie, sealing carefully to edge of pastry shell. Bake 12 to 15 minutes or until golden brown. Cool. Chill thoroughly.

*Use only Grade A clean, uncracked eggs.

1. Beat egg whites and cream of tartar to *soft peaks* before adding sugar.

2. *Gradually* add sugar, beating until *stiff* but not dry. Mixture should be glossy.

3. Spread meringue, sealing carefully to edge of pastry shell.

4. Brown meringue as directed. Cool *slowly*.

INDEX